PRAYERS THAT AVAIL MUCH®
for Your Family

James 5:16

By Germaine Copeland

And this is the confidence that we have in him, that, if we ask anything according to his will, he heareth us: and if we know that he hear us, whatsoever we ask, we know that we have the petitions that we desired of him.

1 John 5:14,15

Harrison House LLC
Tulsa, Oklahoma

16 15 14 13 12 11   10 9 8 7 6 5 4 3 2 1

Prayers That Avail Much for Your Family
ISBN 10: 1-60683-194-1
ISBN 13: 978-1-60683-194-6
Copyright © 2011 by Germaine Copeland
1140 Brannon Drive
Greensboro, Georgia 30642

Published by Harrison House Publishers
P.O. Box 35035
Tulsa, Oklahoma 74153
www.harrisonhouse.com

Contents

Part IV: Prayers for Parenting

Part V: Prayers for Children and Grandchildren

Part VI: Personal Prayers

Introduction

God created the heavens and the earth, and then He made man and woman. He wanted a family that would be the foundation of society. When we look around us we see corruption and sin running rampant and the family structure is in danger of being destroyed. (But God!) We don't have to conform to the world's standards; we can teach and train our children in the ways of God. My parents didn't just tell us about Jesus, but they called us to a Family Altar morning and night, and lived a life that was pleasing to the Lord. They worshiped God with their children present, and commended us to His grace.

Usually my dad, Rev. A. H. "Buck" Griffin, did all the praying and when he was away my mother led us in prayer at the family altar. We always prayed the Lord's Prayer together. There were certain scriptures my dad prayed every time. His nighttime benediction was "LORD, we love You and thank You for the angel of the LORD that encampeth round about our home to protect us and keep us safe." These words are emblazoned on the walls of my heart and have comforted me throughout my lifetime of ups and downs...of rebellion and surrender. There is a promise: Train up a child in the way he should go: and when he is old, he will not depart from it. (Proverbs 22:6.)

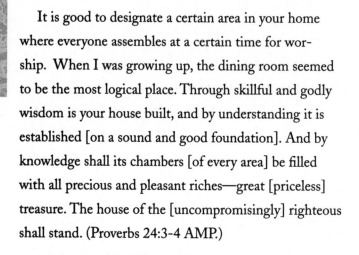

It is good to designate a certain area in your home where everyone assembles at a certain time for worship. When I was growing up, the dining room seemed to be the most logical place. Through skillful and godly wisdom is your house built, and by understanding it is established [on a sound and good foundation]. And by knowledge shall its chambers [of every area] be filled with all precious and pleasant riches—great [priceless] treasure. The house of the [uncompromisingly] righteous shall stand. (Proverbs 24:3-4 AMP.)

One of the fundamental activities you can establish in your home is the family altar. The family altar is a place where you affirm the Lordship of Jesus, keeping Him the center of the home. "[Jesus] is the head of the body, the church; he is the beginning and the firstborn from among the dead, so that in everything he might have the supremacy" (Colossians 1:18 NIV).

Society would mold the minds of your children in this ever changing world. But here in this busyness we live in, make the time for the family altar where you acknowledge that God himself is the source of Life and He has a perfect plan for each of your children. Speak the priestly blessing over your family…spouse and children.

"The LORD bless you and keep you;

the LORD make his face shine upon you

and be gracious to you;

the LORD turn his face toward you

and give you peace.'"

Numbers 6:24-26 NIV

I encourage you to pray the written scriptural prayers in this book for your family and adapt them to pray with your family. Through precept and example you can teach your children the ways of God and He will bless them and give them a heart to walk in His ways.

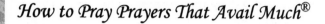

How to Pray Prayers That Avail Much®

The Holy Spirit taught me to pray during a time of crisis in our home, and I have found these principles are effective no matter the situation. The family may be the most difficult school of prayer because here you have to allow the Word of God to divide soul and spirit. You have to yield to the constant ministry of transformation by the Holy Spirit who helps you pray when you don't know how or what to pray. (Romans 8:26-28.)

The drug culture rocked society and the church world was not ready to deal with the demoralizing effects of drug addictions. In his junior year of high school, our son chose the world of drugs and alcohol; I quickly learned my emotional outbursts and fervent emotional prayers were not producing the desired results. My husband and I exhausted our resources, which always left us feeling hopeless.

It became evident that we needed help that only comes from the Throne Room of Heaven, and for a period of time I withdrew from friends and neighbors to inquire of the Lord. As I searched the Scriptures for guidance, the Holy Spirit began teaching me about prayer. Each day I poured out my soul before God, just as Hannah of the Old Testament.

In this book I share the prayers that I prayed and those insights that I learned, sometimes, in very painful circumstances. Needing to know how to pray for my children I turned to the Scriptures and inserted their names in appropriate places.

Praying Scriptures filled with God's promises is a powerful prayer principle. God's Word is His will and by praying what He says in His Word, we can be confident we are praying God's will. The Old Testament prophet, Isaiah, confirms God's Word will accomplish its purpose. (Isaiah 55:11.) Every promise in the Bible belongs to the children of God. If we can find the promise in God's Word, we can pray it over our lives and the lives of others in faith.

The prayers in this book are written from Scripture promises and although they are not all inclusive of every promise, they are a beginning. Praying these prayers changed my life as I submitted to the constant ministry of transformation by the Holy Spirit. (God is not finished with me yet.) The prayers are for you, your personal life, and your family and for others. As you meditate on these promises and pray them aloud, allow the Holy Spirit to make the Word a reality in your heart—believe what you say as you pray. Sometimes it is necessary to persuade your mind that God's Word is

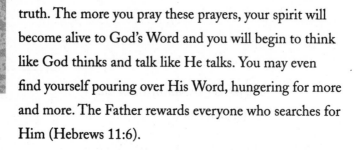

truth. The more you pray these prayers, your spirit will become alive to God's Word and you will begin to think like God thinks and talk like He talks. You may even find yourself pouring over His Word, hungering for more and more. The Father rewards everyone who searches for Him (Hebrews 11:6).

When you seek God, skillful *and* godly wisdom shall enter into your heart, and knowledge shall be pleasant to you. Discretion shall watch over you, understanding shall keep you (Proverbs 2). Wisdom will direct you to believers who will pray in agreement with you; people who will not judge or criticize. There are many "Job's comforters" out there just waiting for an opportunity to correct and let you know where you are missing it and why this calamity has befallen your family. In my experience, many were free to analyze where my husband and I failed…that if we had enough faith our son would be walking with the Lord. (To this day I find it interesting that those who were so free with their words either didn't have children or their children were very young.) But God who is faithful, led me back to James 5:16.

You can take these written prayers a step further by researching the meaning of each Scripture and contemplating the spiritual significance of each verse listed. You may want to look up other promises to add depending on your situation.

Prayer is Communication and Relationship with God

There is nothing more important than spending time in the Word of God and in prayer. To know the Word is to know God. John 1:1 says the Word and God are One. The prayers in this book are a guide for you to have a more intimate relationship with your Heavenly Father because they are full of God's Word. The study of the Scriptures transforms your mind and lifestyle. As you pray and begin receiving answers from your Father, it will reaffirm how much He loves and cares for you. Your desires will begin to change and you will look for ways to please and be a blessing to Him. You will cease trying to instruct God and give Him counsel concerning how to answer your prayers. As you pray according to His Word, He joyfully hears that you—His child—are living and walking in the truth (3 John 4).

Every prayer you have prayed in agreement with God's will for your loved ones is there in the Throne Room of God's grace. Revelation 5:8 speaks of heavenly beings in God's throne room holding the prayers of God's people. It is exciting to know your prayers are

forever in the throne room. God honors your prayers and holds them as precious, just as He sees you as His precious child.

Praying in Faith

God already knows your need, but for Him to answer your prayer you must ask. Jesus says: "Very truly I tell you, my Father will give you whatever you ask in my name…. Ask and you will receive, and your joy will be complete" (John 16:23-24 NIV).

Ask in faith. Ask God for the salvation and deliverance of your children that He might be glorified. When you ask, ask in faith according to the promises given to you: "This is the confidence we have in approaching God: that if we ask anything according to his will, he hears us. And if we know that he hears us—whatever we ask—we know that we have what we asked of him" (1 John 5:14-15 NIV).

Stay in faith by anchoring your soul in what the Scriptures promise: "Do not throw away your confidence; it will be richly rewarded" (Hebrews 10:35 NIV).

Allow the Holy Spirit to lead your prayers. He may bring another Scripture to your remembrance or move you to pray something specific about your situation.

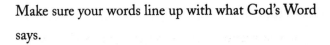

Make sure your words line up with what God's Word says.

Make a decision to praise and thank God. Then praise God for the victory now even though you don't see the answer yet and continue to thank Him for His promises. Walk by faith and not by sight (2 Corinthians 5:7). The Holy Spirit taught me not to discuss the problems. The words you speak carry life or death and I learned when I needed to process, God had someone available who knew how to help me. "Confess to one another therefore your faults (your slips, your false steps, your offenses, your sins) and pray [also] for one another, that you may be healed and restored [to a spiritual tone of mind and heart]. The earnest (heartfelt, continued) prayer of a righteous man makes tremendous power available [dynamic in its working]." (James 5:16 AMP). Look for qualified believers who will help you work through the emotions to the truth that will heal and make you free to move on.

Don't be moved. Satan may tempt you with fear, pain, or a bad report—resist the temptation to speak negatively or rescind what you have asked in faith. James 1:2-4 encourages, "When troubles come your way, consider it an opportunity for great joy. For you know that when your faith is tested, your endurance has a chance to grow.

So let it grow, for when your endurance is fully developed, you will be perfect and complete, needing nothing" (NLT).

Use the armor of God. Ephesians 6:10-18 instructs you to put on the whole armor of God including the belt of truth, the body armor of God's righteousness, and the shoes of the Gospel of peace that prepare you for everything. "Hold up the shield of faith to stop the fiery arrows of the devil. Put on salvation as your helmet, and take the sword of the Spirit, which is the word of God. Pray in the Spirit at all times and on every occasion. Stay alert and be persistent in your prayers for all believers everywhere" (6:16-18 NLT). This is spiritual armor to prepare you for the spiritual battle you face in prayer and in everyday life. Meditating in these Scriptures keeps you spiritually strong not only for your prayer time, but for the rest of your day.

The Bible says we *can* overcome the attacks of the enemy. "He canceled the record of the charges against us and took it away by nailing it to the cross. In this way, he disarmed the spiritual rulers and authorities. He shamed them publicly by his victory over them on the cross" (Colossians 2:14-15 NLT).

Satan is a defeated foe because Jesus conquered him, but he will tempt you to believe otherwise. He is a liar and you can win by not giving up:

- Satan is overcome by the blood of the Lamb (Jesus Christ) and the word of your testimony—what you say matters (Revelation 12:11). Speak God's Word boldly and courageously concerning your situation.

- Fight the good fight of faith and resist the temptation of unbelief (1 Timothy 6:12).

- Withstand the attacks in your thoughts and be firm in faith—rooted, established, strong and determined. "Stand firm against him, and be strong in your faith. Remember that your Christian brothers and sisters all over the world are going through the same kind of suffering you are" (1 Peter 5:9 NLT).

- Run with endurance the race God has set before you by keeping your eyes on Jesus, the Champion who initiates and perfects your faith (Hebrews 12:1-2 NLT).

- God is always with you and will give you what you need to overcome: "Now I'm turning you over to God, our marvelous God whose gracious Word

can make you into what he wants you to be and give you everything you could possibly need in this community of holy friends" (Acts 20:32 MSG).

I praise God that in the name of Jesus prayer is limitlessness. It belongs to every child of God. Commit yourself to pray about situations right away, and to pray the best way—by approaching God with your mouth filled with His Word and your heart open to His Spirit. That's what these prayers are all about!

Watch Your Words

James 5:16 says the prayers of a righteous person are powerful and effective. Once you begin delving into God's Word, you'll find your words are very important— not just in your prayer time, but all the time. As you pray and believe for a situation, to then talk negatively about it will cause you to doubt your prayer did any good. Psalm 50:23 reveals those who are thankful and praise God will see His salvation. That's the best possible re- sponse to any situation you have committed to prayer— thanksgiving and praise.

The book of James also says to be a doer of the Word and not just a hearer—a hearer who does noth- ing deceives himself (1:22). Those who do what the

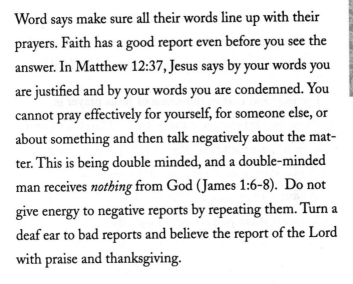

Word says make sure all their words line up with their prayers. Faith has a good report even before you see the answer. In Matthew 12:37, Jesus says by your words you are justified and by your words you are condemned. You cannot pray effectively for yourself, for someone else, or about something and then talk negatively about the matter. This is being double minded, and a double-minded man receives *nothing* from God (James 1:6-8). Do not give energy to negative reports by repeating them. Turn a deaf ear to bad reports and believe the report of the Lord with praise and thanksgiving.

In Ephesians 4:29-30, MSG it says:

> Watch the way you talk. Let nothing foul or dirty come out of your mouth. Say only what helps, each word a gift. Don't grieve God. Don't break his heart. His Holy Spirit, moving and breathing in you, is the most intimate part of your life, making you fit for himself. Don't take such a gift for granted.

Reflect on these words and give them time to keep your perspective in line with God's will. Our Father has much, so very much, to say about that little member, the tongue:

- Take control of your words: "The tongue also is a fire, a world of evil among the parts of the body.

It corrupts the whole body, sets the whole course of one's life on fire, and is itself set on fire by hell" (James 3:6 NIV).

- Give the devil no opportunity by getting into worry, unforgiveness, strife, or criticism: "Therefore each of you must put off falsehood and speak truthfully to your neighbor, for we are all members of one body. 'In your anger do not sin': Do not let the sun go down while you are still angry, and do not give the devil a foothold" (Ephesians 4:25-27 NIV).

- Avoid gossip and foolish talking: "Obscene stories, foolish talk, and coarse jokes—these are not for you. Instead, let there be thankfulness to God" (Ephesians 5:4 NLT).

- You are to be a blessing to others: "Therefore, whenever we have the opportunity, we should do good to everyone—especially to those in the family of faith" (Galatians 6:10 NLT).

Talk the answer, not the problem. The answer is in God's Word. Strive to gain knowledge of that Word—revelation knowledge as mentioned in 1 Corinthians 2:7-16. You are free to believe God's Word! The Holy Spirit, your Teacher, will reveal the things that have been freely given to you by God—precious promises for your situation. The Holy Spirit wants to help you if you will take the time to listen in your spirit. God sent Him to you for that purpose (John 14:26).

Unite in Prayer

Avoid the gossipers and critics! As a believer and an intercessor, unite with others in prayer at every opportunity. United prayer is a mighty weapon that the Body of Christ is to use. Matthew 18:19 says, "If two of you agree here on earth concerning anything you ask, my Father in heaven will do it for you" (NLT). What a powerful promise! In Hebrews 10:24-25, the Scriptures encourage believers to meet together: "And let us consider how we may spur one another on toward love and good deeds, not giving up meeting together, as some are in the habit of doing, but encouraging one another" (NIV).

Praying for Others

The prayers in this book that are personal may also be used as intercessory prayers for others simply by praying them in the third person, changing the pronouns "I" or "we" to the name of the person for whom you are interceding and then adjusting the verbs accordingly. Remember that you cannot control another's will, but your prayers prepare the way for the individual to hear and understand truth.

Ministry to Others

As you come into a closer relationship with God and a greater understanding of God's Word through prayer, others may notice a change in your life and come to you seeking advice. You may not know the exact answer to their need, but as you lead them to the Word of God, you can be confident the Father will minister to them just as He has to you.

Be a person of integrity and purpose to walk in God's counsel and prize His wisdom in all the affairs of life (Psalm 1; Proverbs 4:7-8). People are looking for something on which they can depend. When someone in need comes to you, share the Scriptures that provide the answer to their problem. Psalm 112 says of the righteous that even in darkness, light dawns for you—you who are gracious and compassionate. Your heart is secure and steadfast, trusting in the Lord. Blessed are those who trust the Lord and find delight in His Word.

How Often Should I Pray?

An often-asked question is: "How many times should I pray the same prayer?"

The answer is simple: You pray until you know the answer is fixed in your heart. After that, you need to repeat the prayer whenever adverse circumstances or long

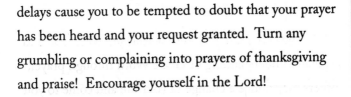

delays cause you to be tempted to doubt that your prayer has been heard and your request granted. Turn any grumbling or complaining into prayers of thanksgiving and praise! Encourage yourself in the Lord!

The Word of God is your weapon against the temptation to lose heart and grow weary in your prayer life. When that Word of promise becomes fixed in your heart, you will find yourself praising, giving glory to God for the answer, even when the only evidence you have of that answer is your own faith. Reaffirming your faith enforces the triumphant victory of our Lord Jesus Christ.

Vain Repetitions

There was another question that sent me in search of truth. Over time I began to hear teachings on prayer. I thank God for everyone I agreed with and for those with whom I disagreed because they both inspired me to study with an open mind…a mind alert to error and alert to truth. The following question was one that created many hours of study. Our son was still out there living in the pig sty and eating "husks." I needed to know how long was I to pray the same prayers for him. When we repeat prayers more than once, aren't we praying 'vain repetitions'? I didn't want to do anything that would hinder my intercession for our son!

The Holy Spirit taught me the truth in this matter and I am so grateful. This is referring to the admonition of Jesus when He told His disciples: "And when you pray, do not use vain repetitions as the heathen *do*. For they think that they will be heard for their many words" (Matthew 6:7 NKJV). Praying the Word of God is not praying the kind of prayer that various religions pray—a kind of formula or chant. It is the Living Word of God—alive and full of power (Hebrews 4:12). The Message Bible says Matthew 6:7 like this: "The world is full of so-called prayer warriors who are prayer-ignorant. They're full of formulas and programs and advice, peddling techniques for getting what you want from God. Don't fall for that nonsense. This is your Father you are dealing with, and He knows better than you what you need."

First Kings 18:25-39 lists various manners of prayer offered to false gods, and people of other religions are still doing this in our modern society. Elijah invited the false prophets of the pagan god Baal to call fire down on an altar to prove to the children of Israel that the Lord God was the only true God. The false prophets shouted, danced around their altar, and cut themselves until evening. Then Elijah built an altar of stone, put a sacrificial bull on the altar, and covered the sacrifice with water—so much that there was a mote full of water around the altar. After he prayed a short prayer, the Lord sent fire down from heaven and burned up the sacrifice and all the water, even in the mote. The Lord is not impressed by long prayers full of eloquent words, He is impressed with a heart after God who believes in His Word.

The prayers in this book are written from the Holy Scriptures—they are not vain words. They are spirit and life and mighty through God to the pulling down of the strongholds of the enemy (2 Corinthians 10:4-6). You have a God whose eyes are over the righteous and whose ears are open to your prayer; when you pray, He hears (Psalm 34:15). Every time you repeat Scriptural prayer you are reinforcing the triumphant victory of Jesus!

You were made righteous in Christ Jesus when you accepted Him as your Lord and your prayers will avail much. This word "righteous" simply means that you are now rightly related to God the Father. These prayers will bring salvation to the sinner, forge a pathway for the prodigal to return home, bring deliverance to the oppressed, healing to the sick, and prosperity to the poor. They will usher in the next move of God on the earth. In addition to affecting outward circumstances and other people, your prayers will also affect you. In the very process of praying, your life will be changed as you go from faith to faith and from glory to glory.

What Is Prayer?

The earnest (heartfelt, continued) prayer of a righteous man makes tremendous power available [dy-
namic in its working].

–James 5:16 AMP

In the quietness of the cool autumn day I gazed upon
the beauty of creation, and considered the ways of the
perfect formation of geese as they went by my window.
This is part of my prayer, my meditation as I contem-
plate God's handiwork. If only my life were so orderly.
I am a spirit learning to live in a world where there are
trials and tribulations. Praying has become a major part
of who I am.

People ask me to define prayer. Prayer is fellowshipping with the Father—vital, personal contact with God.
As your Heavenly Father and your Friend, He is truly
more than enough. For every situation, He has an answer; for each heartache, He has restoration; for sickness,
He has a healing. Where relationships have fallen into
disarray, He has peace and contentment. Determine to
stay in constant communion with Him—talk to Him in
your spirit throughout your day, listen for His direction,
and do what He leads you to do.

> The eyes of the Lord are upon the righteous (those
> who are upright and in right standing with God), and
> His ears are attentive to their prayer....
>
> 1 Peter 3:12 AMP

Resist the temptation to turn prayer into a religious form with no power. It is intended to be effective and accurate and bring *results*. Jeremiah 1:12 says God watches over His Word to perform it. An important part of effective prayer is to pray God's promises over the situation, understanding that He will watch over His Word to make sure it happens.

> The word of God is alive and powerful. It is sharper
> than the sharpest two-edged sword, cutting between
> soul and spirit, between joint and marrow. It exposes
> our innermost thoughts and desires.
>
> Hebrews 4:12 NLT

Scriptural prayer is this "living" Word in your mouth. When you pray God's Word, you are speaking faith and it takes faith to please God (Hebrews 11:6). As you hold His Word up to Him in prayer, He sees Himself in His Word.

God's Word is your contact with your Heavenly Father. You are putting Him in remembrance of His

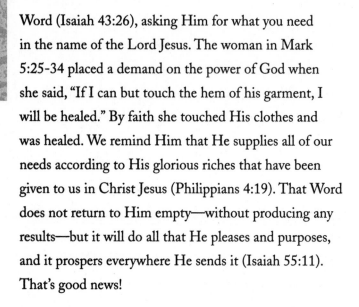

Word (Isaiah 43:26), asking Him for what you need in the name of the Lord Jesus. The woman in Mark 5:25-34 placed a demand on the power of God when she said, "If I can but touch the hem of his garment, I will be healed." By faith she touched His clothes and was healed. We remind Him that He supplies all of our needs according to His glorious riches that have been given to us in Christ Jesus (Philippians 4:19). That Word does not return to Him empty—without producing any results—but it will do all that He pleases and purposes, and it prospers everywhere He sends it (Isaiah 55:11). That's good news!

God did *not* leave us alone without His thoughts and His ways because we have His Word—His bond. God instructs us to call on Him, and He will answer and show us great and mighty things in our future (Jeremiah 33:3). Prayer is an exciting journey of faith—not a bother.

Prayer is Crucial

As a Christian, your first priority is to love the Lord your God with your entire being and your neighbor as yourself (Mark 12:30-31). Loving God includes getting to know Him through prayer. All believers are called to pray—it is your avenue of fellowshipping with your Fa-

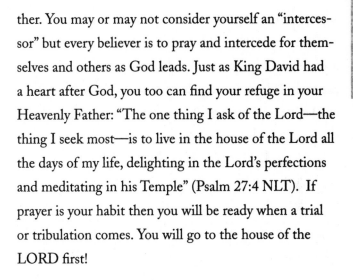

ther. You may or may not consider yourself an "intercessor" but every believer is to pray and intercede for themselves and others as God leads. Just as King David had a heart after God, you too can find your refuge in your Heavenly Father: "The one thing I ask of the Lord—the thing I seek most—is to live in the house of the Lord all the days of my life, delighting in the Lord's perfections and meditating in his Temple" (Psalm 27:4 NLT). If prayer is your habit then you will be ready when a trial or tribulation comes. You will go to the house of the LORD first!

The importance of knowing God personally is found throughout the Bible, but one passage in the New Testament makes it so clear. Jesus speaks of things unbelievers worry about—what to eat, what to wear—and encourages His disciples not to be concerned with those things: "But seek first his kingdom and his righteousness, and all these things will be given to you as well" (Matthew 6:33 NIV).

When you take time to pray in faith believing in God's Word, you are seeking His kingdom and His righteousness and God brings your requests to pass. You hear Him more and more clearly as you renew your mind to the Word of God. He says His eyes search the whole earth to show Himself strong in behalf of those who are

totally committed to Him (2 Chronicles 16:9 MSG).
In Christ you are made holy and blameless. You are His
very own child (Ephesians 1:4-5). He tells you to come
boldly to the throne of grace and receive mercy and find
grace to help in your time of need (Hebrews 4:16). You
have an open invitation to talk to your Father any time
and as much as you want. He wants to hear from you.

The Art of Prayer

The prayers in this book are designed to teach and
train you in the art of prayer. There are many different
kinds of prayer, such as the prayer of thanksgiving and
praise, the prayer of dedication and worship, and the
prayer that changes *things* (not God). It may be that God
changes you and you change things. These various kinds
of prayers are included in this book and categorized for
you to learn how to pray in each situation.

As you pray scripturally, you will be reinforcing the
prayer armor, which you have been instructed to put on
in Ephesians 6. "Put on the full armor of God, so that
you can take your stand against the devil's schemes" (v.
11 NIV). The fabric from which the armor is made is
the Word of God: the belt of truth, the breastplate of
righteousness, the shoes of readiness that come from the
gospel of peace, the shield of faith, the helmet of salva-

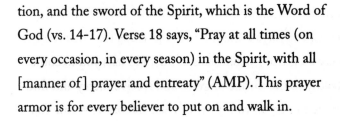

tion, and the sword of the Spirit, which is the Word of God (vs. 14-17). Verse 18 says, "Pray at all times (on every occasion, in every season) in the Spirit, with all [manner of] prayer and entreaty" (AMP). This prayer armor is for every believer to put on and walk in.

Second Corinthians 10:4-5 reveals another reference to the battle you face in prayer: "We use God's mighty weapons, not worldly weapons, to knock down the strongholds of human reasoning and to destroy false arguments. We destroy every proud obstacle that keeps people from knowing God. We capture their rebellious thoughts and teach them to obey Christ" (NLT). This is spiritual warfare and it takes place in your mind as you pray and as you become a doer of the Word

In 1 Timothy 2 we are admonished that, "…petitions, prayers, intercession and thanksgiving be made for all people— for kings and all those in authority, that we may live peaceful and quiet lives in all godliness and holiness. This is good, and pleases God our Savior, who wants all people to be saved and to come to a knowledge of the truth" (1 Timothy 2:1-4 NIV). *Prayer is the responsibility of believers and it is important to our Heavenly Father.*

Prayer must be your foundation. Jesus says you are to live by every Word that proceeds from the mouth of God

(Luke 4:4). Desire the whole counsel of God because it has the ability to bring positive changes to your life. By receiving His counsel through the Word, you will be "… transformed (changed) by the [entire] renewal of your mind [by its new ideals and its new attitude], so that you may prove [for yourselves] what is the good and acceptable and perfect will of God, even the thing which is good and acceptable and perfect [in His sight for you]" (Romans 12:2 AMP).

It may well be true that any failure is really a prayer failure. In prayer is where you receive direction, is where you develop confidence that God hears you. Learning to wait on Him to give you the wise answer requires patience. No believer should have to live apart from God's blessings—ignorant of God's Word. God desires for His people to be successful, to be filled with a full, deep, and clear knowledge of His will (His Word) and to bear fruit in every good work (Colossians 1:9-13). That is how you bring honor and glory to Him (John 15:8). He desires for you to know how to pray, for "the prayer of the upright is his delight" (Proverbs 15:8).

Using the Word of God in Prayer

Using God's Word on purpose, specifically, in prayer is one kind of prayer, and it is a very effective and accurate method. Jesus says, "The words (truths) that I have been speaking to you are spirit and life" (John 6:63 AMP).

When Jesus faced Satan in the wilderness, He said, "It is written…it is written…it is written." You are to live, be upheld, and be sustained by every word that comes from the mouth of God (Matthew 4:4).

James, by the Spirit, says you do not have because you do not ask. You ask and don't receive because you ask with wrong motives (James 4:2-3 NIV). That's a strong word! Strive to become an expert in prayer—learn to ask God and evaluate your motives. When you spend consistent time in the Word and in prayer, you will be able to correctly explain and handle the Word of Truth (2 Timothy 2:15 NLT). You will gain a greater understanding of how to pray the Word over your situations.

Using the Word in prayer is *not* taking it out of context—His Word in you is the key to answered prayer—to prayer that brings results. When you pray He "…is able to do exceedingly abundantly above all that we ask or think, according to the power that works in us" (Ephesians 3:20 NKJV). The power lies within God's Word. It is anointed by the Holy Spirit. The Spirit of God does not lead you apart from the Word; the Word is of the

Spirit of God. Apply that Word personally to yourself and to others—not adding or taking from it—in the name of Jesus. Apply the Word to the *now*—to those things, circumstances, and situations facing you *now*.

When you use God's Word in prayer, it is not something you just rush through, uttering once. There is nothing "magical" or "manipulative" about it—no set pattern or device in order to satisfy what you want or think out of your natural mind. Instead, you are holding God's Word before Him. Jesus said for you to ask the Father in His name. Ask and believe, expecting His divine intervention (2 Corinthians 4:18).

The Holy Spirit is Our Helper

The Father has not left you helpless. Not only has He given you His Word, but also He has given you the Holy Spirit to help you in your weakness when you don't know how to pray (Romans 8:26 NLT). The Holy Spirit is a divine helper, and He will direct your prayer and help you pray when you are struggling. Our Father has provided His people with every possible avenue to ensure their complete and total victory in this life in the name of our Lord Jesus (1 John 5:3-5).

Pray to the Father, in the name of Jesus, through the Holy Spirit, according to the Word.

The Prayers of Paul

Paul was very specific and definite in his praying. The first chapters of Ephesians, Philippians, Colossians, and 2 Thessalonians are examples of how Paul prayed for believers. There are numerous others. *Search them out.* Paul wrote under the inspiration of the Holy Spirit. You can pray these Spirit-given prayers today; they are powerful and effective.

In 2 Corinthians 1:11, 2 Corinthians 9:14, and Philippians 1:4, you see examples of how believers prayed one for another—putting others first in their prayer life with *joy.* Your faith works by love (Galatians 5:6). You grow spiritually as you reach out to help others—praying for and with them and holding out to them the Word of Life (Philippians 2:16).

The Word of God Changes You

Man is a spirit, he has a soul, and he lives in a body (1 Thessalonians 5:23). In order to live a successful Christian life, you should take care of each of these three parts. Your body needs food and water for physical strength. The soul, or intellect, needs intellectual stimulation to continue to learn, develop, and stay alert. But it is the spirit—the heart or inward man—that is the real you, the part that has been reborn in Christ Jesus. It must have

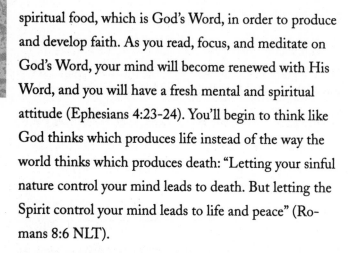

spiritual food, which is God's Word, in order to produce and develop faith. As you read, focus, and meditate on God's Word, your mind will become renewed with His Word, and you will have a fresh mental and spiritual attitude (Ephesians 4:23-24). You'll begin to think like God thinks which produces life instead of the way the world thinks which produces death: "Letting your sinful nature control your mind leads to death. But letting the Spirit control your mind leads to life and peace" (Romans 8:6 NLT).

In the same way you renew your mind, you can also present your body as a living sacrifice: "Give your bodies to God because of all he has done for you. Let them be a living and holy sacrifice—the kind he will find acceptable. This is truly the way to worship him. Don't copy the behavior and customs of this world, but let God transform you into a new person by changing the way you think. Then you will learn to know God's will for you, which is good and pleasing and perfect" (Romans 12:1-2 NLT).

Refuse to let your physical body or your soul (your natural mind, will, and emotions) dominate your decisions. The very best for your body and soul is to be in subjection to the spirit man where there is life and peace (1 Corinthians 9:27). In Proverbs 4:20-22 you find that

God's Word is healing and health to our natural man: "Listen carefully to my words. Don't lose sight of them. Let them penetrate deep into your heart, for they bring life to those who find them, and healing to their whole body" (NLT). God's Word affects each part of you— spirit, soul, and body. You become vitally united to the Father, to Jesus, and to the Holy Spirit—one with Them (John 16:13-15; John 17:21; Colossians 2:10).

Purpose to hear, accept, and welcome the Word. As you learn to believe the Word, speak the Word, and act on the Word, you'll find it is a creative force. Not only does it change circumstances, but it also changes you. The Word is a double-edged sword—often placing a demand on you to change attitudes and behaviors toward the person for whom you are praying!

Many people agree that the Bible is true, but do not do what it says; they are mental assenters. *Real faith is acting on God's Word now.* Sometimes faith is purposing in your heart to believe what you are saying and some- times it is an action God leads you take. Without prac- ticing the Word you cannot build your faith. To develop an active prayer life, God's Word actually has to be a part of your life. "In the same way, faith by itself, if it is not accompanied by action, is dead" (James 2:17 NIV). The Lord Jesus is in heaven presenting your prayers to the

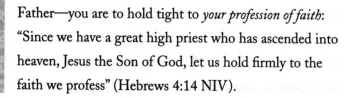

Father—you are to hold tight to *your profession of faith*: "Since we have a great high priest who has ascended into heaven, Jesus the Son of God, let us hold firmly to the faith we profess" (Hebrews 4:14 NIV).

Meditation

Prayer does not cause faith to work, but faith causes prayer to work. Any prayer problem is a lack of knowledge or a problem of doubt—doubting the integrity of the Word and the ability of God to stand behind His promises or the statements of fact in the Word. But this can be resolved by preparing your heart.

You can spend fruitless hours in prayer if your heart is not prepared beforehand. Preparation of the heart or the spirit comes from meditation on the Father's Word, meditation on who you are in Christ, and what He is to you. It is the same for you just as God told Joshua (Joshua 1:8), as you meditate on the Word day and night and do according to all that is written, you will make your way prosperous and have good success. Attend to God's Word, submit to His sayings, keep them in the center of your heart, and put away contrary talk (Proverbs 4:20-24).

Prayer based upon the Word rises above the senses, contacts the Author of the Word, and sets His spiritual laws into motion. It is not just saying prayers that brings results, but it is spending time with the Father, learning His wisdom, drawing on His strength, being filled with His quietness, and receiving His love.

In this book there is a section of personal confessions. These Scriptures are set-aside for you to meditate on and say over your life on a regular basis. When you speak them out, they clear the negative thoughts the enemy brings—thoughts that you are unworthy and powerless. The truth contained in these Scriptures will build your inner being and strengthen your faith to believe and not doubt God's Word. Don't let the lies of the enemy or the cares of this life hold back your prayer life. Discover the person God has made you in Christ Jesus and begin the wonderful adventure of prayer. You have the power to deliver your loved one out of a strange land!

Personal Confessions

I love the Lord my God with all my passion and prayer and intelligence, and I love others as well as I love myself.' (Matthew 22:37-39 MSG.)

Jesus is Lord over my spirit, my soul, and my body. (Philippians 2:9-11.)

I am God's child. He sent Christ Jesus to save me, to make me wise, acceptable to God, and holy. I can do all things through Christ who strengthens me. (1 Corinthians 1:30 CEV, Philippians 4:13.)

The Lord is my Shepherd. I have all that I need. God supplies all my needs from His glorious riches, given to me in Christ Jesus. (Psalm 23 NLT; Philippians 4:19 NLT.)

I do not worry or have anxiety about anything, instead I pray about everything. God cares for me so I turn all my worries over to Him. (Philippians 4:6 NLT; 1 Peter 5:7 WE.)

I am the Body of Christ. I am redeemed from the curse, because Jesus bore my sickness and carried my diseases in His own body. I was and am healed by His wounds. I forbid any sickness or disease to exist in my body. Every organ, every tissue of my body works in the perfection in which God created it to work. God bought me with a high price and paid for my healing. I honor God and bring glory to Him in my body. (Galatians 3:13; Matthew 8:17; 1 Peter 2:24 KJV, NLT; 1 Corinthians 6:20 NLT.)

I have the mind of Christ and hold the thoughts, feelings, and purposes of His heart. I think as Christ thinks. (1 Corinthians 2:16 AMP, WE.)

I am a believer and not a doubter. I hold on to my declaration of faith. I decide to walk by faith and practice faith. My faith comes by hearing, and hearing by the Word of God. Jesus is the Author and Developer of my faith. (Hebrews 4:14 GW; Hebrews 11:6; Romans 10:17; Hebrews 12:2.)

God's love has been poured out in my heart by the Holy Spirit who has been given to me. His love abides in me richly. I keep myself in the Kingdom of light, in love, in the Word; God holds me securely and the evil one cannot touch me. (Romans 5:5; 1 John 4:16; 1 John 5:18 NLT.)

God has given me authority to trample on snakes and scorpions and to overcome all the power of the enemy; nothing will harm me. My faith is like a shield and I

stop all the flaming arrows of the evil one. God's Spirit in me is greater than the devil that is in the world. (Luke 10:19 NIV; Ephesians 6:16 GW; 1 John 4:4 NCV.)

I am delivered from this present evil world. I am seated with Christ in heavenly places. I reside in the Kingdom of God's dear Son. The law of the Spirit of life in Christ Jesus has made me free from the law of sin and death. (Galatians 1:4; Ephesians 2:6; Colossians 1:13; Romans 8:2.)

I do not fear. God has not given me a spirit of fear and timidity, but a spirit of power, of love, of self-control and a sound mind. God is on my side. (2 Timothy 1:7 NLT, KJV; Romans 8:31.)

I hear the voice of the Good Shepherd. I hear my Father's voice, and the voice of a stranger I will not follow. I roll my works upon the Lord. I commit and trust them wholly to Him. He will cause my thoughts to become agreeable to His will, and so my plans will be established and succeed. (John 10:27; Proverbs 16:3.)

I am a world overcomer because I am born of God. I represent the Father and Jesus well. I am a useful member in the Body of Christ. I am God's masterpiece, recreated in Christ Jesus to do good works God prepared in advance for me. It is God Who works in me to will and to act in order to fulfill His good purpose. (1 John 5:4-5; Ephesians 2:10 NLT, KJV, NIV; Philippians 2:13 NIV.)

I let the Word of Christ dwell in me richly in all wisdom. He Who began a good work in me will continue until the day of Christ. (Colossians 3:16, Philippians 1:6.)

From David's Heart

Mom and Dad,

Thank you for standing for me while I ran from God as fast and as far as I could. Through alcohol, drugs, jail time, failed marriages and just a lifestyle of bad choices, decisions and addictions, you never gave up on me. I am so thankful for the two of you and that both of you stood on God's unfailing Word for me. I could never thank you enough. I know that I am truly blessed. Even when you were moved by circumstances emotionally, you continued to believe God and His Word for my eternal redemption. I believe it was your prayers, along with all the others that God raised up to come alongside you, that gave me ears to hear God speak to me! As you know God asked me to "choose this day life or death." I chose life and I am here today. I love you, Mom and Dad. Thank you so much.

~David

PART I:

OUR FAMILY'S STORY

Praying for Your Children

It is winter but the day is warm and sunny with a
slight breeze blowing. The well-dressed couple standing outside the prison gates is obviously uncomfortable. They wait with others who are passing the time
in conversations that reveal they have been here before.
The drama is much too real as the electric gates slide
open. Taking deep breaths and with heads held high,
they begin walking toward the entrance of the cold, drab
building.

A smiling stranger introduces herself and walks
alongside the retired couple, explaining the procedure for
visiting behind the gray concrete walls. After submitting
their drivers' licenses, they enter the noisy room filled
with metal chairs, where clusters of people sit leaning
toward each other. Armed guards walk the periphery of
the visitors' quarters arranging chairs as the large room
fills up.

Men's faces light up as they walk through the guarded
door and reach out for those who are waiting to see
them—girlfriends, parents, wives, infants, and children.
Staking out three metal chairs, the mother listens to the
subdued greetings, tears, and laughter—observing the

total lack of privacy. Her heart grieves as she absorbs what this brief visit means to the incarcerated whose eyes are riveted on their friends and family.

Lonely people grasping for a few moments of togetherness surround her. She wishes she could talk with the teenager wearing the Georgia Tech shirt, a familiar site, but strangers keep their eyes averted—careful not to make eye contact with anyone outside their space. The mother's life will never be the same. It was easy to sit in her office reading mail and praying for faceless prisoners who were far away—behind walls she never expected to enter.

The reality of the moment hits hard as the guard opens the door. The couple's son, dressed in prison garb, walks toward them and after exchanging hugs they pull the three cold metal chairs closer in a semi-circle. The parents haven't driven over two hours for small talk, and they begin to explore the why, where, when, and how did they get here.

The silence of many years is broken as the three discuss their hurts, anger, and frustrations—opening the door for healing and recovery. The reticent father reveals some of his innermost feelings, and the son notes they haven't talked like this in thirty years.

Much too soon, my husband and I have to say good-bye to our cherished son.

Wayward Children

I am a PK—a preacher's kid. Over my lifetime I saw my peers choose different paths; some followed in their parents' footsteps while others denied their faith and walked away to the dismay of mothers and dads. My sister, two brothers, and I went our separate ways; at one time my older brother declared himself an atheist, but one by one we returned to the God of our childhood. Through many challenges, my parents believed God who gave precious promises concerning children: "Train up a child in the way he should go [and in keeping with his individual gift or bent], and when he is old he will not depart from it" (Proverbs 22:6 AMP).

It's always a difficult situation in any family when a child goes astray, especially when addiction seems to be the major issue. Parents wonder where they failed and how this could happen to them. Just as other ministers have done, there were times our dad judged himself according to 1 Timothy 3:5: "For if a man does not know how to rule his own house, how will he take care of the church of God?" (NKJV). When our children became teenagers, my husband and I too, had to consider this passage of Scripture.

In our family we had to deal with not only a rebellious teenager, but also an addiction. Addiction is not just an individual issue; it is a family problem—a time for soul searching—a time to embrace the Word that is able to save the individual's soul. If a PK leaves the paths of righteousness, the parents feel their ministry is discredited and they usually suffer in silence. In some cases they become so concerned about their own reputations they go to great lengths to keep their situation a secret, but addictions are hard to contain.

Emotions Released in Prayer

Today, many families are touched by addictions. Every encounter with school authorities, counselors, and police ignites the hope that this time their child will truly repent and turn from their evil ways. When authority is rejected again and again, feelings of failure, shame, anger, grief, guilt, disappointment, and betrayal assail the parents, interfering with their prayers. They don't feel like praying. How could their child do this to them—how could God let this happen?

In the midst of heartache, parents can identify with Old Testament saints who poured out their anguish to God. Their prayers were not beautifully written—they were prayers of wretchedness and grief. Job said, "I will speak out in the anguish of my spirit, I will complain in the bitterness of my soul" (7:11 NIV). This is not the time to run from God but the time to run to the One who can somehow make bitter experiences sweet.

You will need prudence, wisdom, and discernment from God to make decisions concerning the wayward child. You must know when to let go and let God. Many times it appeared my husband and I were talking to our son, only to find we were heard and answered by the addiction. *Your children shall be disciples taught of the Lord* (Isaiah 54:13) is a statement we tend to ignore, convinced if we tell them one more time they will get it! "Taught of the Lord" often escapes us and we gravitate toward "taught of Mom and Dad."

Even though some would condemn us for showing emotions, we read on more than one occasion King David prayed through his anguish and frustration. In Psalm 56:8 he prayed, "You've kept track of my every toss and turn through the sleepless nights, every tear entered in your ledger, each ache written in your book" (MSG). In 1 Samuel 1-2, Hannah poured out her emotions before God. The priest who mistook her emotional outpouring for drunkenness did not distract her. She knew her God would answer her prayer. The Apostle James confirms

this when he says, "The effective, fervent prayer of a righteous man avails much" (James 5:16 NKJV).

Praying for Your Adult Children

How do you stand in faith for your wayward child? When you are in the midst of a crisis what do you do? Before your emotions get out of control, pour yourself out before God. He gave you emotions as a release. On an occasion when I was very distraught about a situation, I began to weep bitterly feeling broken. Finally, the sobbing subsided and I heard the voice of my Father, "You may be broken, but you are not crushed. I can put you back together."

Over the years of standing for our son's deliverance from a lifestyle of addictions, the Lord has taught me some vital truths. Below are brief summaries of lessons I learned pouring over my children in prayer. My hope is that you will remember them when you are struggling and avoid difficult setbacks.

- Refuse to harbor self-pity. It only hurts you and can hinder your faith. Trust that God knows how to turn your situation for good just as He promises in Romans 8:28.

- Submit to the constant ministry of transformation by the Holy Spirit and receive the salvation of your soul. I'm not referring to the salvation of your spirit when you accept Jesus Christ as your Lord, but the transformation of your mind, will, and emotions—elements that make up your soul. The transformation of your soul is a process you walk out. When it comes to your children, the temptations for worry, anxiety, guilt, anger, and frustration may be great but by submitting to the counsel of the Holy Spirit, He will fill you with peace and help you to stay in faith.

- Study and learn all you can about addictions—the Holy Spirit will help you. I read many books and attended a group session for nine months where I gained insight into family dynamics. The Holy Spirit exposed and analyzed soulish areas of my life that needed to be transformed—an unexpected blessing even though at the time it was trying.

- Not only should you pray but also become an example to your family as you exchange wrong, ungodly thinking for God's thoughts. Thought patterns (positive or negative) control relationships and behavior. Your thoughts will be exhibited when you speak and your family will be listening.

- Avoid denial and do not cover up the sin—stay away from the blame game.

- Allow the transgressor to walk out his or her consequences. Too often parents rush to fend off accusers, pay fines, blame others, make excuses, and interfere with rehabilitation programs by rescuing the transgressor before the process is completed.

- Forgive—forgive yourself for your mistakes and forgive your child for his or hers. God is not holding anything against you; you hold the thoughts, feelings, and purposes of His heart (1 Corinthians 2:16 AMP). Choose to go with God's leading, for His way is always perfect for your child. There is no sin that your child can commit that is beyond God's forgiveness. Is anything too hard for God?

- Let go of preaching "at" them and refuse to judge and condemn them. They know what you believe, and being in your presence brings condemnation—not from you, but from their own conscience! Jesus said let him who is without sin cast the first stone (John 8:7). Your children are disciples *taught of the Lord* (Isaiah 54:13) so let Him teach them.

- Listen with discernment when they talk to you, rather than thinking about what you can say that will turn the situation around. I am reminded of something I heard attributed to Dr. Billy Graham:

"It's God's job to judge, the Holy Spirit's job to convict, and our job to love." You must first love the Lord your God, then be willing to connect to a fresh understanding of the grace of God for your child and yourself.

- Pray according to the Word and in the Spirit. Once you put the law of prayer into operation, do not turn coward or lose heart. God loves your child even more than you do and He needs you to intercede when they are struggling.

- Build up the hedge of protection through prayer and continue to stand in the gap before the Father crying out for mercy on behalf of your wayward child. Mercy will triumph over judgment. Your prayer makes way for God to interpose the influence of His Spirit on the heart and mind of this one who has lost their way. God is faithful—when you commit yourself to Him, you and your family will be saved.

In Luke 22:31 we see Jesus as our example. He said to Peter: "Simon, Simon, Satan has asked to sift all of you as wheat. But I have prayed for you, Simon, that your faith may not fail. And when you have turned back, strengthen your brothers" (NIV).

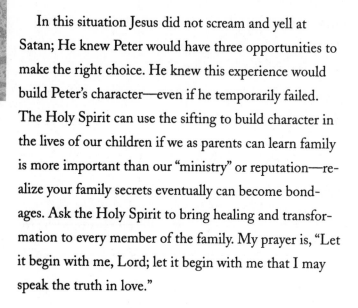

In this situation Jesus did not scream and yell at Satan; He knew Peter would have three opportunities to make the right choice. He knew this experience would build Peter's character—even if he temporarily failed. The Holy Spirit can use the sifting to build character in the lives of our children if we as parents can learn family is more important than our "ministry" or reputation—realize your family secrets eventually can become bondages. Ask the Holy Spirit to bring healing and transformation to every member of the family. My prayer is, "Let it begin with me, Lord; let it begin with me that I may speak the truth in love."

Unconditional Love

We are taught God is love, but to truly experience His salvation in our destitute state is the most wonderful thing in the world. Everyone's experience with God is unique to their life because He loves each of us as an individual precious child. The book of Psalms says, "Blessed (happy, fortunate, to be envied) is he who has forgiveness of his transgression continually exercised upon him, whose sin is covered" (Psalm 32:1 AMP). Once we experience the grace of being forgiven and unconditionally loved, our hearts are made new and we able to love others in the same way. We are to be envied by the world not necessarily because of our wealth or status, but because of our love for our Lord and each other. "By this everyone will know that you are my disciples, if you love one another" (John 13:35 NIV). Because of our son David's traumatic experiences when he was far from God and the amazing unconditional love God demonstrated to him, David is at a place now where he can speak from his heart:

> Jesus loved enough to where when He knelt to pray
> in the Garden of Gethsemane and was under so
> much stress that his sweat was as beads of blood, He
> still determined to sacrifice his life for our redemp-
> tion. Medically it has been proven that this can
> happen—under great stress the capillaries under the
> skin can actually burst and bleed as sweat. That's how
> grieved Jesus was about what was going to happen.
> He could have said to the Father, "I've been down
> here and these people aren't worth it." But that was
> not His response. This is the same love He gave to
> us and when the world sees the love that we have for
> one another, they're going to want it. I know there
> are many countries that send missionaries to America
> now—they send missionaries to America because
> many in America are lost. And those lost are ready
> to experience this love—it's about a relationship with

Him. Every time a soul gets saved, they rejoice in heaven. We've just got a little inkling of it, but it's a love that will last for all time, for eternity.

David's hope is to help others avoid the destructive lifestyle he lived, full of bitterness and unforgiveness. David says only God can work true forgiveness in us. There may be times in relationships, with children, parents, or a spouse, when as humans we cannot forgive—but God in us can if we're willing to let Him. "We are not responsible for all the things that happen to us," David adds. "When bad things happen to us, they happen; there's nothing we can do about it. But we are 100 percent responsible for our reaction to it. Are we going to forgive? Are we going to let God come in there with His surgical knife? Because that's what He does, He comes in and He cuts those things out. And when He cuts them out, He can fill us with His love. Then we can take that love and give it away to the next person; that's what this life is all about."

Praying for Your Loved Ones

Isaiah 35 is prophecy about the coming Messiah—Jesus Christ—and now that He has come and redeemed us, these verses are very powerful to pray over you and your family. David and I pray these Scriptures for our

children, grandchildren, spouses, and ourselves. As I
share from these verses from the perspective of a parent,
David adds his insight from the perspective of both a
parent and a child. We'll start from Isaiah 35:3-4:

> Strengthen the weak hands, and make firm the
> feeble knees. Say to those *who are* fearful-hearted,
> "Be strong, do not fear! Behold, your God will come
> *with* vengeance, *with* the recompense of God; He will
> come and save you" (NKJV).

God will strengthen up our knees, strengthen up our
weak hands, because our physical bodies can become
weak and our emotions stressed; we can become weary
and tired, especially when we're praying for someone
close to us and negative reports keep coming back.

Now that David is praying for his own family and
loved ones, he understands what I went through when
he was so far away from God. David says, "When I was
out there dealing dope, my mom kept getting bad news.
Know that when we're praying for someone, there's a
report that's going to come back to us. The enemy will
try everything to make sure that he gets in there, because
then we have a choice to make. *Am I going to believe
what God says about him or her?* You know in Isaiah
54:13 it says my children are disciples taught of the Lord

and they are obedient to God's will, not my will: 'And all your [spiritual] children shall be disciples [taught by the Lord and *obedient to His will*], and great shall be the peace and undisturbed composure of your children' (AMP). Is that what our response is going to be? Or are we going to run to sister so-in-so or brother so-in-so and say, you know my son's out there doing this, my daughter's out there doing that? That just puts us in agreement with the enemy. We're going to be in agreement with one or the other and we've got to realize that. We really have to stay strong in faith and watch what we say over our children."

Isaiah 35 continues to speak of our redemption through Christ:

Behold, your God will come *with* vengeance; with the recompense of God. He will come and save you. Then the eyes of the blind shall be opened, and the ears of the deaf shall be unstopped. Then shall the lame man leap like a hart, and the tongue of the dumb shall sing for joy. For waters shall break forth in the wilderness and streams in the desert.

Isaiah 35:4-6 AMP

This Scripture shows God himself will come and save our children. It's not our job to be their savior, but we can pray and by standing in gap for our children, we give God an avenue to work in their life. David says it like this, "That's what I'm doing; I'm taking the Word of God and praying it over my children, over my loved ones—even over myself. I pray the eyes of the blind will be opened. Their blind eyes will be opened. I can't do it. I can't open their ears, but He can. From verse five I pray: 'Their deaf ears will be unstopped, the walls will come down, and they'll hear the voice of God. They'll hear the voice of the Good Shepherd and they will run to it (John 10:3-4). The lame or where they are lame—in the areas they are weak and fallen—they will leap as deer. And the tongue of the dumb shall sing and rejoice for God.'"

Isaiah 35 finishes with these verses:

> For waters shall break forth in the wilderness and streams in the desert. And the burning sand and the mirage shall become a pool, and the thirsty ground springs of water; in the haunt of jackals, where they lay resting, shall be grass with reeds and rushes. And a highway shall be there, and a way; and it shall be called the Holy Way. The unclean shall not pass over it, but it shall be for the redeemed; the wayfaring men, yes, the simple ones and fools, shall not err in it and lose their way. No lion shall be there, nor shall

any ravenous beast come up on it; they shall not be found there. But the redeemed shall walk on it. And the ransomed of the Lord shall return and come to Zion with singing, and everlasting joy shall be upon their heads; they shall obtain joy and gladness, and sorrow and sighing shall flee away.

Isaiah 35:6-10 AMP

These Scriptures reveal God's mighty promises of deliverance for your children when they are in the wilderness far from Him. God himself will break through the dry and thirsty places with living waters. For that wayward son or daughter, God will bring streams of living water in their desert. God will come and rescue them. David likes to pray, "Holy Spirit, wash them, wash them. And then their parched ground shall become a pool of living water. And their thirsty land will be springs of water."

In verse seven the Scripture refers to the "haunt of jackals" and in another translation, this is referred to as "the habitation of dragons" or demons. This means where demons have made their home—where the enemy has had a hold in your child's life—now there is redemption; fresh grasses, reeds, and rushes will spring forth. The life of God will come up from them. David adds,

"Because I'm speaking the Word of God over them, it will never ever return void (Isaiah 55:11). It's never, ever failed—God's Word has never failed. The answer might not have come when we wanted it to, but His Word still never failed."

After standing in faith for David for more than 25 years, that is a statement I can confirm. Your faith can stand the test of time. Just don't give up.

This passage ends with God making a way for your child to find the truth. "And a highway shall be there, and a way; and it shall be called the Holy Way. The unclean shall not pass over it, but it shall be for the redeemed; the wayfaring men, yes, the simple ones and fools, shall not err in it and lose their way" (35:8 AMP). I love the way David prays this passage:

> And my (child) children will walk the highway of holiness and any unclean thing shall be cut off and it will not pass over it, but they will walk over that highway. And the wayfaring men, though they make foolish decisions, they will not make a mistake and lose their way. God will put them back on the highway. God will get them where He needs them to be.

David adds, "That's my prayer for my children now and God has given me more promises for them. As I

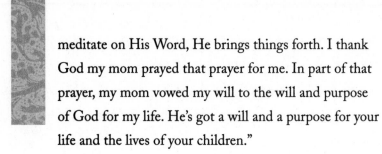

meditate on His Word, He brings things forth. I thank God my mom prayed that prayer for me. In part of that prayer, my mom vowed my will to the will and purpose of God for my life. He's got a will and a purpose for your life and the lives of your children."

Your Child Has a Destiny

After 28 years of addictions, my son, David, was delivered from alcohol, drugs, and dealing drugs. He is now
a remarkable Christian man. He serves the Lord as vice
president in charge of operations and grounds for Word
Ministries. God not only saved David but also David's
destiny. It was not in my timing but God's. He knew
exactly what it would take for David to be delivered and
God was willing to wait. We often want answers to our
prayers immediately, but some things take time. God
is faithful to fulfill His promises and we must stand
strong in faith. When you ask David about his journey
to freedom he responds, "It's about relationships. It's all
about giving the love of the Father. I was given that love
and now I'm standing for loved ones. I can't go back and
undo anything that's been done, but what I can do is
hopefully share with people where I came from so they
won't have to go through that kind of pain."

Imaginations

Many times our minds can try to take us down the
wrong path when we are standing for loved ones. We
have to take hold of our thoughts and bring them into
the obedience of Christ as the Apostle Paul tells us in

2 Corinthians 10:5. When it comes to our children, we have to think and speak God's Word over them instead of the circumstances we see in the natural. This can be difficult without God's help. David says, "One of the things I ask God for is godly imaginations. The Bible speaks of those who listen to lying vanities and give place to destructive imaginations; they forsake the mercy of God. I ask Him to give me godly imaginations concerning my loved ones. Give me a vision. Because I guarantee you when God gives you a vision, it will not matter what anyone says—you already know the final outcome. You know they're going to be there in heaven with you. And you'll get to that point just like my mom did, and just like I've done with my children; it doesn't really matter whether I see it here or not. Oh, it'll be grand and glorious if I do—I'll rejoice, I'll dance, I'll shout. But as long as they're with me in heaven, as long as they're with me through eternity, then it's going to be okay. They'll be with Jesus."

No Condemnation

When a child goes astray, as a parent, you are tempted to condemn yourself for past mistakes and take the blame for your child's shortcomings. We must not forget in our natural state we are not perfect, but thankfully

God sees us through the perfect blood of Jesus. His grace forgives our mistakes. We cannot live the abundant life God has provided for us under the clouds of guilt from the enemy. We raise our children in the admonition of the Lord and when they grow up, they have to make decisions for themselves. As I mentioned earlier, God promises if we train our children up to know the Lord, they will return to Him when they are older (Proverbs 22:6). If you did not raise your children to know the Lord, you are still not at liberty to live under condemnation; when you accept Jesus as Lord, you are redeemed and inherit the blessings of God. Find the promises in God's Word that you can anchor your faith in and stand on them. Acts 16:31 and Joshua 24:15 are verses you can declare over your loved ones for their salvation no matter how they were raised.

Healing from Hurts

For a child who has returned to the Lord, it can be helpful for them to realize the challenges they faced and where they made poor choices. For David, this was especially beneficial. He responds, "When each one of you were born, the world was changed. Now, it's up to you to choose how it changes—more light or more darkness. And it's up to us which path we choose. I chose darkness. I chose darkness for thirty years—walked in it. The reason I chose darkness was that I refused to deal with things that happened to me."

God revealed to David that he harbored hurts from his childhood—things I did not even imagine would have hurt him. David explains, "When I was almost three years old, my parents had another baby and Renae was brought into the world. My mom went to the hospital and I was sent down to my grandparent's house. And you know, I always loved to go down there. But Grandmother and Gramps decided they were going to bring me up to see the baby before we left. They carried me up to the hospital and showed me this newborn baby. Then they whisked me off to Florida. As a little guy that told me I was being replaced. I had been replaced. Did anybody intentionally do that? No, of course not. My parents loved me; my daddy would have laid down his life for me. My mom would have done anything for me. But at that age, that was one main thing I heard inside."

Even as young children, we can begin to build up walls to protect ourselves from hurt and rejection. David, from a very young age, began to build these walls. The enemy is right there with deception to keep families divided in an attempt to tear them apart and steal the joy and security of the family bond. That's why we pray the

Word over our children all of their lives—it sets a hedge of protection around them from the deceit of the enemy.

Another area the enemy used against David was his relationship with his father. Looking back David can see his father was not perfect, but certainly not against him. As a child, however, his false perception was his reality. David recounts one incident in particular:

One of the strongholds I built up at the age of eight or nine started when I was playing Little League baseball. Our team had made it to the Little League World Series. At that time we had the National League and the American League. If you were in the National League you could not pitch if you were nine years old, only eight-year-olds could pitch—that was the rule. But if you were in the American League, you could pitch at eight or nine—it didn't matter.

Well, my dad was the coach of our National League team and one thing about my dad is a rule is a rule. Laws are laws and that's just the way it is.

I knew the boy pitching for the American League and he was nine years old, and I did everything I could to get my dad to let me pitch. He couldn't do it and he wouldn't do it. So I built up another wall because I thought even if unfair laws didn't apply to

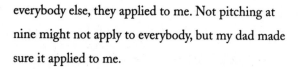

everybody else, they applied to me. Not pitching at nine might not apply to everybody, but my dad made sure it applied to me.

David could have learned a different lesson from his dad—a lesson of how important it is to be honest, but as a child he internalized this incident as a form of rejection. There are hurtful things we will experience in this life that God uses for our good. Whether we put ourselves in situations, the enemy brings something against us, or God allows things to take place, God always knows how to turn them for our good. David says, "I've learned God can take our pain and He can take our hurt, and He can fix it."

The book of Hebrews speaks of the chastisement of the Lord—the ones God loves, He chastises. "In other words when we start getting off the path a little ways, God's going to let some things happen to us," David comments, "and hopefully it'll move us back on the path. He's going to chastise us; He's going to prune us and the reason He does it is so that we can go forth and bear more fruit." In our natural state, we need the discipline of the Lord, and even if it feels uncomfortable at the time, God works in us His glory:

We have had earthly fathers who disciplined us and we yielded [to them] and respected [them for training

us]. Shall we not much more cheerfully submit to the
Father of spirits and so [truly] live? For [our earthly
fathers] disciplined us for only a short period of time
and chastised us as seemed proper and good to them;
but He disciplines us for our certain good, that we
may become sharers in His own holiness.

Hebrews 12:9-10 AMP

The chastisement of God is good and He is able to
turn bad situations for our good, but He does not send
bad situations. He does not teach us by putting sickness
on us or sending some type of evil to our door. The one
who instigates evil is Satan—the enemy of our soul. The
Bible is very straightforward about God's intentions:
"When people are tempted, they should not say 'God is
tempting me.' Evil cannot tempt God, and God himself
does not tempt anyone" (James 1:13 NCV). God is good
and loves us. He would not do anything to hurt us. James
1:17 says: "Every good thing given and every perfect gift
is from above, coming down from the Father of lights,
with whom there is no variation or shifting shadow"
(NASB).

Generations of Problems

When David was ten years old, my husband's father
passed away. Everette, my husband, had problems that

were passed down by his father and David recognized those struggles. David remembers, "My grandfather was an alcoholic, the same problem I had. He was an addict. Back then they didn't call it alcoholism, but I remember my granddaddy would lie in bed and he had his bottle of liquor and his little shot glass. He drank it until it killed him. That's what my dad saw, so he had his own walls. He had his own issues he had to deal with. We all have our own issues, our own problems we've got to deal with, but we have to deal with them.

"When my grandfather died I remember standing there crying. I looked up and I saw my dad—he didn't shed a tear. My dad could not shed a tear for his father. He's since dealt with that issue. He wrote his dad a letter, went to his grave, and read it. Later he let me read the letter. But at the time of my grandfather's death, I made up my mind I was going to make my father cry. I was going to and I succeeded in doing that through my addictions. I started looking at pornography when I was 13 years old. I started smoking marijuana at the age of 15, and by 16 I was drinking. I did it a little backwards— most people get into drinking, then drugs—I got into drugs and then drinking. It doesn't really matter; an addict is an addict. Now I'm still an addict—I'm addicted to God."

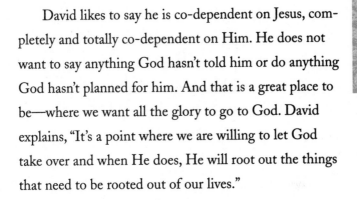

David likes to say he is co-dependent on Jesus, completely and totally co-dependent on Him. He does not want to say anything God hasn't told him or do anything God hasn't planned for him. And that is a great place to be—where we want all the glory to go to God. David explains, "It's a point where we are willing to let God take over and when He does, He will root out the things that need to be rooted out of our lives."

Remembering his grandfather's passing and as a husband and father, David knows how important it is for men to show emotions. David relates, "I was raised most of my life with men who did not show emotions. Well that idea is a lie straight from the pit of hell. Our children need to see us weep and they need to see us on our knees. When we come home and our families are together, we need to take the time to get around one another be thankful to God. Thank God we all made it back home safely, that we have homes to live in, and food to eat. Let's give God the glory. When our children see the Light of God in their homes that Light will go forth intensified and darkness will be dispelled."

When you walk into a dark room and flip on the light switch, you don't have to cast the darkness out because the light dispels it. David says, "Let's get on with the

Light. Let's get on with love. Let's show our children exactly what they need to see, and they'll rise up. When I was in prison and praying, God told me He is raising up a generation that will be as radical for Him as Marilyn Manson is for the devil. God is raising them up and we need to be a part of that."

Everyone Needs to Feel Valuable

Children need to feel loved and valued by their parents. Sometimes as parents we are so busy with our own lives, we don't take the time to focus on how our children feel about themselves. When David was about 16, he began to really struggle in this area. He wanted to be "somebody." Everette always tried to help David by showing him ways he could do things better, but David took that as harsh criticism—as if he was a failure to his father. Everette, on the other hand, always wanted his father to instruct him—to help him better himself. So to Everette, he was giving his son exactly what he thought his son would want—that's how Everette expressed his love for David.

David recalls, "As a child, when I would have an excellent baseball game or a winning football game, I would come off thinking I had done great job. Then all of a sudden, my dad would tell me about the one tackle

I missed. Or he might say I should have been playing a little deeper, or a little closer, or this or that. I didn't hear any love in that. I didn't feel my dad was proud of me."

That left a hole in David. He needed to feel valued—that he belonged—and at that time of his life, he did not know who he was in Christ. He did not have a strong enough relationship with God to anchor his soul and he sought out other ways to fill the void. David began selling drugs and found a false sense of security in this new identity. "I became known as Dr. Dope—that's what people called me," David says. "I was the man. I was the one everybody wanted to run to because I made sure I had the best dope that was available."

David recalls his spiral downward:

> I had people that would pick up in Miami, run all the way up into New York dropping off, and come back down the coast collecting their money. I could make one phone call and have 1,500 pounds, no problem. And when I was 17 years old, I found out about strip bars. At that time you weren't supposed to get in until you were 21, but they didn't kick out too many people with big rolls of hundred dollar bills in their pocket, especially when they're willing to go and sit down with bottles of champagne. I found those women ac-

tually flattered me. They talked me up and made me really feel good—they really did. But, of course, it was only because I was spending all my money. And I fell into that trap—a big vicious circle. I was dealing dope and I had a wife and three children. If you opened my refrigerator you would find food and dope.

Eventually that led to getting robbed. Five men broken into our house—they held my wife and me at gunpoint. They actually carried us in the bedroom. They tied me up and put me on the floor, and put her on the bed. Now you can imagine what our thoughts were, but someone was praying. I had a mom at home and she had an unction from the Holy Spirit to pray. She was on her knees praying Psalm 91—the covering of protection. She was praying out about the covering—God's covering. And it just so happened they took my wife off the bed, tied her up beside me, took our wedding rings, took all of our jewelry, took anything that they could pick up and carry off, and they put a blanket over us. My mom was praying for a covering, and they put a blanket over us! Yes, God has a sense of humor.

Still Searching

The robbery scared David straight but not into the arms of Jesus. He was still searching for his identity in his own strength. He gave up the life of drinking and drugs and began going to church. I was thrilled—I thought it was an answer to prayer and it was, just not the answer I expected. God knows the human heart and what it takes to bring His children back to His heart.

David was in church and studying his Bible but it was for all the wrong reasons. It was still about David receiving the praise and approval of men. David says, "My attitude was, *God, what are you going to do for me?* I still had all those issues and problems. All the big preachers who were going somewhere with God read their Bibles and prayed at least an hour day—that's what I heard. I mean that's the way I saw it. So that's what I started doing. But I didn't do it to get intimate with my Father. I didn't do it to draw nigh to Him. I didn't do it to run and jump up into His lap. I did it for my glorification. I did it so that others would look to me—let healing go forth, let the anointing go forth, because *I'm* here—not because Jesus is here. That kind of pride doesn't work in the kingdom of God."

David became tired in his own efforts. The Christian life is really impossible without the help of the Holy Spirit. It is in Christ we live and move and have our being (Acts 17:28). David emphasizes, "You try doing this on your own and you're going to get burned out. This natural body is not made to do it; this mind is not made to do it except in God. That's the reason we've got to get that light down on in the inside. When we are born again, that's what happens—the light of God comes into our spirit. But if we have walls built up like I did, God wants to start tearing those walls down. He starts pulling them down, piece by piece just as we built them up piece by piece. I didn't give Him a chance to work in me. I was trying to do it myself with all those problems and issues still there."

It is an important process to let God work in our lives, heal our hurts, and make us whole again. Especially for wayward children, we have to be patient and give God time to finish the work in them.

A Stranger Once Again

For six years, David kept searching for something to fulfill him even after he made a decision to live for Christ. He was worn out. In his weakness he turned to one of his old friends and for a fix. David remembers, "I just had a beer and a joint the first time and I thought, *I can handle this.* Then the second time, I had a few more beers—I still felt like I was in control. But within three months I was back drinking and doing drugs on a regular basis." David felt like a stranger when he was with his

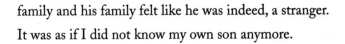

family and his family felt like he was indeed, a stranger. It was as if I did not know my own son anymore.

During this time David maintained a successful business but his addiction continued to worsen. When he received his fourth DUI ticket, he was sentenced to a prison term. It was a hardship on all of us, but I had to trust in God and remember the Scriptures that promise He would work this for David's good (Romans 8:28-30).

Finally Broken

When David's wife asked for a divorce on her second visit to the prison, David felt as if his life was falling apart. He first turned to the "dope man" in prison to block out his hurts, but God came to him and spoke, "This day choose life or choose death." David was shaken to the core—he knew it was his last chance. With his life in shambles, David laid everything at the feet of Jesus. David says, "I believe God speaks those words to every person at some point in their life, but it was the prayers of my mom and other family that paved the way for me to hear God's voice."

While David was in prison I questioned whether he was doing well or not, but when Everette and I visited him, we saw a change in his demeanor. There was a new

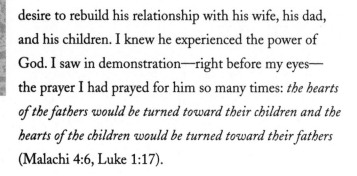

desire to rebuild his relationship with his wife, his dad, and his children. I knew he experienced the power of God. I saw in demonstration—right before my eyes— the prayer I had prayed for him so many times: *the hearts of the fathers would be turned toward their children and the hearts of the children would be turned toward their fathers* (Malachi 4:6, Luke 1:17).

Accountable to God

David's journey is one of running from God—for 30 years he ran from God. As he reflects on his actions, he knows he was accountable to God during those years. "I had an encounter with God when I was 12 years old and I was saved. I have no doubt I was saved at that time. I'm not a theologian but from experience I can tell you, if God would've come back during those years I was away from Him I don't think He would have taken me. I was not abiding in the vine, I was cut off, and I was turned over to a reprobate mind."

David was taught of the Lord and I knew he was saved at a young age. Yet, he had to choose Christ for himself. I had my own journey of dealing with a wayward child and I found that God knows best how to bring one of His own home. As a parent, our position is to be accountable for doing what God directs—pray,

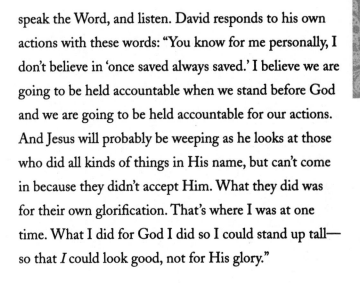

speak the Word, and listen. David responds to his own actions with these words: "You know for me personally, I don't believe in 'once saved always saved.' I believe we are going to be held accountable when we stand before God and we are going to be held accountable for our actions. And Jesus will probably be weeping as he looks at those who did all kinds of things in His name, but can't come in because they didn't accept Him. What they did was for their own glorification. That's where I was at one time. What I did for God I did so I could stand up tall—so that *I* could look good, not for His glory."

Abiding in Christ

Abiding in Christ is much more than just reading your Bible and reciting prayers. We can be so close to Him—closer than a best friend, closer than a spouse. He is always with us and in us, desiring to encourage and bring hope to us. David says, "He wants to wrap His arms around us when we're hurting. When a test or trial comes our way or when we get hurt, we should run to God, fall down on our faces, and ask Him what our attitude should be. Ask if He is giving us an opportunity. We need to find God's will when we are hurting."

God is able to take your negative circumstances and turn them around. You can search for His will or you can depend on yourself, but things work out so much better when you follow His direction. David explains, "See there's self and there's God. Jesus died for all our sin and all He asks of us is to die to self—die to our self-will, die to trying to do everything in our own strength. When we do that, we will value the person beside us as much as God does. When we realize it's about His will for our lives and we let Him shine, the emotional walls and barriers will start falling down. He'll start tearing them apart and we can become whole. We have a Daddy who says, 'My son, My daughter, you're precious to Me.'"

Consequences and Grace

David and his wife were divorced while he was in prison, and it was at this point that David fully turned his life over to God. David explains, "My wife told me that she was going to file for divorce. And when you're in prison, there's not much you can do about it, especially when the phone is cut off and you can't contact anyone. So I would sit down on my bunk and I'd say, 'Okay God, here's my marriage, here's my life, here's my family—I give it to You.' Sometimes I had to do it six, eight, ten times a day. But I did it and I left it in His hands."

When David was released from prison, he reconciled with his wife and they were remarried. It seemed like a miracle, but old issues resurfaced and eventually they divorced again. David struggled with this especially since he was living his life for God. David says, "I'm not here to tell you that once you get saved you're going to have an easy life or once you give it to God everything's going to be roses, because it's not. You will still have problems, but it's just what you do with them. Are you going to keep your eyes on the problems or on God?"

In Matthew 14 the disciples have taken their boat out and a storm has arisen. They see Jesus coming to them walking on the water. Peter calls out to Jesus and says, "Lord if it's you...tell me to come to you on the water" (Matthew 14:28). But when Peter sees the waves, he begins to sink and calls for Jesus to save him. Jesus catches him and responds, "You of little faith...why did you doubt?" (Matthew 14:31). God taught David a powerful truth from this passage that he relates to his marriage. He explains, "Who failed in that boat? Did Peter fail by getting out of the boat and sinking? Or did the other eleven fail by staying in the boat? It was real comfortable in the boat—they were safe and sound. It might have been storming but they had already been out there most of the night and they knew if they stayed in the boat they would be safe. But Peter said to Jesus, 'If you say, then I'll get out of the boat.' That's where we should be.

Step out in the waters that are rough—step out in the areas that hurt. And as long as we keep our eyes on Jesus, we'll walk through. We'll get through the storm. But when we start saying, 'There's a problem! I can't do this.' That's when we start sinking. And then Jesus reaches down and pulls us back up. He's faithful. He knows who we are and that we're going to make some wrong choices. That's grace. He allows for our shortcomings."

David stood for his marriage to be restored for four years but eventually God released him. David responds, "Studying the Scriptures during this time helped me. We all have choices to make and I cannot make a choice for others, only myself."

Coming fully to Christ took a long time for David and there were consequences. But today he speaks of God's grace from his own experience and healing: "You cannot look to your spouse, your girlfriend or boyfriend to make you whole. No one person can take the place of God. You become whole in God first and then when you link up with a brother or sister, it's a threefold cord and just like Ecclesiastes 4:12 says, a threefold cord is not easily broken. Then you're talking about prayers that will be answered and walls that will be torn down. Great things will come forth, because you are whole and you are in unity."

The Anointing on Families

Your family may seem dysfunctional at times, but there is an anointing on godly families. In the book of Exodus, God appointed Aaron, Moses' brother, as the high priest. His family was appointed as priests unto God and his tribe, the Levites, were appointed as priests. Only the Levites were to minister to the Lord with sacrifices for the people of Israel. But after Jesus came, those who come to God through Him are anointed as priests and kings unto God (Revelation 1:6). We are to minister to the Lord ourselves. We are to have a close, intimate relationship with our heavenly Father.

There is a priestly anointing upon godly families just as there was upon Aaron and his family. That anointing acts as a covering for you and your family—bringing the blessings of God to generation after generation including peace, joy, prosperity, and healing. The enemy, however, wants to steal that anointing from you and your family. Since David lived outside of our family anointing for many years, he has a real understanding of how powerful it is to live under God's blessings. He relates:

> My father loved me—no doubt about it, but he never ever said, "I love you." And most men in his generation don't say those words. That's just something that

has been eliminated. I see the work of the enemy and he has a plan just like God has a plan, but his plan is for our destruction (John 10:10). And that's what he is trying to do; he's trying to destroy families because of the anointing on them, just as it was on Aaron and his family. Aaron was anointed as priest and then he passed it down to his sons. And that is what we're supposed to do—we are anointed as priests and we are to pass it down to our children.

Men, you are the priest of your house; you are the priest of your home. What are you passing down? What are your children seeing? Are you preparing the next generation to stand up and fight for God? Or are you so caught up in work that your children believe work is more valuable than they are? A lot of us get to that point, at least, I know I did. We have a responsibility to train up our children to know God and His ways. We all want our children to have good lives and the way that happens is to live for God, let His blessings overtake us, and teach our children to do the same.

Perhaps you are the first in your family to live for God—then let it start with you. The anointing and blessings of God can start with your family.

Shining Lights

David has come to the point where he welcomes
God's work in his life. He realizes the value of letting
God take down the walls of unforgiveness and bitterness.
He wants to be what God wants him to be and do what
God asks him to do. He says, "We can all get to that
point. I'm no better than anybody else. We are all valu-
able in God's eyes."

David's oldest son is involved with mentoring young
adults on leadership. David couldn't be more proud. "It's
just great the things he's doing," David exclaims. "He is
involved with young kids and mentoring them on leadership. That's what we've got to have—the Body of Christ
has to have leaders. We are the shining light; we are not
the darkness. We are the shining light that's supposed
to go forth with the love of Jesus. We are to be ministers
wherever we are at. We're all called—every one of you is
called. It doesn't matter where you're at, you are called to
be a light in that area."

Prayer Works

God has beautifully restored David's relationship with
his children, grandchildren, Everette, and me. Everette
and David are the closest they have ever been. And since
David has four children and thirteen grandchildren, I am

so thankful. Yes, that means I have *great* grandchildren
and they are wonderful! When I visited David those
months in prison, I remember David would say that God
would restore his relationships. He knew it wouldn't be
his own efforts, but God's favor. I stand in amazement at
how God has restored our family. Those years of prayer
and intercession made a difference and I'm so thankful
God has given us weapons to fight against the attacks
of the enemy. After 28 years of addictions, David was
delivered. Don't lose hope for your situation. Stay in the
Word and pray it out every day or even several times
a day. Stay in faith and trust God to do the work He
promised.

PART II:

PRAYERS FOR DAILY LIVING

Beginning Each Day

Father, this day belongs to You! I will celebrate and be glad today. It is better to obey than to sacrifice so today, I am making a decision to submit to Your will so that my plans and purposes may be conducted in a manner that will bring honor and glory to You. Help me to be spiritually and mentally alert in this time of meditation and prayer.

I completely trust You and place my family in Your keeping - my parents, spouse, children, and grandchildren – knowing the One I trust is able to guard what I have entrusted to Him. Thank You for ordering Your angels to protect me and my family wherever we go. They will hold us up with their hands so that we won't even hurt our feet on a stone. Thank you, Father that Your love never ends and Your mercy never stops. Your loyalty to me is great!

Father, I kneel in prayer to You – all beings in heaven and earth were created by You. You are wonderful and glorious and I pray that Your Spirit will make us strong followers and that Christ will live in our hearts because of our faith.

You can do anything, Father – far more than we could ever imagine or guess or request in our wildest dreams – by Your Spirit within us. Glory to You forever! Amen

Scripture References

Lamentations 3:22-23 NCV   Psalm 118:24 NCV

Ephesians 3:14-17 NLT   1 Samuel 15:22 NCV

Ephesians 3:20 MSG   2 Timothy 1:12 NLT

Psalm 91:11-12 NLT

To Help Others

Father, in the name of Jesus, I will treat others as I would want to be treated. I want love to be my highest goal! I purpose to make it my aim, my great quest in life.

In the name of Jesus, I will not push my way to the front. I will love others and lend them a helping hand. I purpose to build them up in all ways – spiritually, socially and materially – as I am led by Your Spirit. I desire to imitate You, Father, and encourage others and give them strength.

Father, in the name of Jesus, I will love my enemies and be good to them. I will lend without expecting to be paid back. Then, I will be acting as a child of the Most High who is good to people even who are unthankful and bad.

Thank you, Father, for imprinting Your laws upon my heart and inscribing them on my mind – on my inmost thoughts and understanding. According to Your Word , as I would like and desire that men would do to me, I do exactly so to them, in the name of Jesus. Amen.

Scripture References

Luke 6:31 NLT　　　　　　Philippians 2:4 MSG

Ephesians 6:10 NIV　　　　Luke 6:35,36 WE

Romans 15:2 NIV & AMP　Luke 6:31 AMP

1 Thessalonians 5:11 NCV　Ephesians 5:1,2 AMP

Hebrews 10:16 AMP

1 Corinthians 14:1 NLT, AMP

To Walk in Love

Father, in Jesus' name, I thank You that You fill my heart with love by the Holy Spirit which has been given to me. I keep and treasure Your Word. The love of and for You has truly reached its goal in me; and true love chases all my worries away.

Father, I am Your child and I *commit to walk in the God kind of love.* I will never give up. I care more for others than myself. I don't strut. I don't want what I don't have. I don't force myself on others or think about me first. I don't fly off the handle. I don't keep score of others' sins. I don't revel when others grovel but I take pleasure in the flowering of truth. I put up with anything. I trust God always. I always look for the best, never looking back, I keep going until the end. The love of God in me never dies.

Father, I bless and pray for those who would harm me. I wish them well and do not curse them. Because of this, my love will overflow more and more in knowledge and understanding. I will live a pure and blameless life until the day of Christ's return. I am filled with the fruits of righteousness – the righteous character produced in my life by Christ Jesus.

Everywhere I go I commit to plant seeds of love. I thank You, Father, for preparing hearts ahead of time to receive this love. I know that these seeds will produce Your love in the hearts to whom they are given.

Father, I thank You that as I walk in Your love and wisdom, people are being blessed by my life and ministry. Father, You make me to find favor, respect and affection with others (*name them*).

My life is strong in and built on love, knowing that You are on my side and nothing is able to separate me from Your love, which is in Christ Jesus my Lord. Thank you, Father, in Jesus' precious name. Amen.

Scripture References

Philippians 1:9-11 NLT   Romans 5:5

1 John 2:5 NCV   John 13:34

1 Corinthians 13:4-8 MSG 1 John 4:18 MSG

1 Corinthians 3:6   Daniel 1:9 NLT

Romans 12:14 NCV   Ephesians 3:17 NCV

Matthew 5:44   Romans 8:31,39

1 Corinthians 13:4-8 MSG

To Walk in Forgiveness

Father, in the name of Jesus I make a fresh commitment to You to live in peace – to get along with everybody –with my brothers and sisters of the Body of Christ, with my friends, associates, neighbors, and family.

Father, I repent of holding on to bad feelings toward others. Today I let go of bitterness, rage, anger, harsh words, and slander and all other types of bad behavior. I ask Your forgiveness for the sin of _____. By faith, I receive Your forgiveness knowing that You cleanse me from all the wrongs that I have done. I ask You to forgive and release all who have wronged and hurt me. In the name of Jesus, I forgive and release them, and will show them kindness and mercy just as You have shown me.

From this moment on, I give up my evil ways, and will be gentle and sensitive to others, speaking kind words of encouragement, and I will do what is right. I know that I have right-standing with You, Father, and You watch over everyone who obeys You and You listen to my prayers.

It says in Your Word that Your love has been poured into my heart by the Holy Spirit who is given to me. I

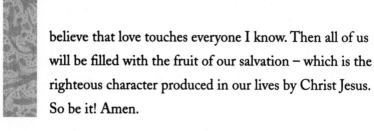

believe that love touches everyone I know. Then all of us will be filled with the fruit of our salvation – which is the righteous character produced in our lives by Christ Jesus. So be it! Amen.

Scripture References

Romans 12:16-18 MSG   Mark 11:25

Romans 12:10   Ephesians 4:32 NCV

Philippians 2:2   1 Peter 3:8,11,12 NCV

Ephesians 4:31 NLT   Colossians 1:10

Ephesians 4:27   Romans 5:5

John 1:9 NCV   Philippians 1:9,11 NLT

PART III:

PRAYERS FOR
RELATIONSHIPS

The Harmonious Marriage

Father, it is written in Your Word that Your love fills our hearts by the Holy Spirit whom God has given to us. Because You are in us, love will grow more and more. Love is more important than anything else. It is what binds us completely together in perfect harmony.

We will live and conduct ourselves and our marriage with honor, esteeming our marriage as precious, worthy and of great price. It is our purpose to honor You by walking in agreement with You and with each other, helping each other fulfill our God-given destinies. Father, we believe and say that we are kind and merciful and forgiving of one another and others. We seek peace that will bring calmness and safety forever – the kind of peace that no one can understand but can only come from You.

Our marriage grows stronger day by day because it is deeply rooted in Your love. Father, thank You that You will make every word that You give us come true in our marriage in Jesus' name. Amen.

Scripture References

Romans 5:5 NCV

Philippians 1:9 NLT

Colossians 3:14 NLT

Colossians 1:10 NCV

Philippians 2:13

Philippians 2:2 MSG

Ephesians 4:32 NCV

Isaiah 32:17 NCV

Philippians 4:7

1 Peter 3:7

Ephesians 3:17,18 NLT

Jeremiah 1:12 MSG

For My Family Members

Thank you, Jesus that You have poured out Your Spirit from heaven upon my family. Our desert will be like a fertile field and the fertile field like a forest. Justice will be found even in the desert and fairness will be found in the fertile fields. That fairness will bring peace, and it will bring calm and safety forever.

Our family lives in peaceful places and in safe homes and calm places of rest. Because we belong to You, Lord, we have stability even in bad times and You provide a rich store of salvation, wisdom, and knowledge. The fear and respect for You, Lord, is our treasure.

Lord, be merciful to us for we have waited for You. Be our strong arm each day and our salvation in times of trouble—trials and tribulations.

Thank You, Father, for being my sure foundation each and every day. I praise You with all of my life! Amen.

<u>Scripture References</u>

Isaiah 32:15-18 NCV   Isaiah 33: 2,6 NLT

To Choose Godly Friends

Father, help me to meet new friends – friends who will encourage me and lift me up. I want to spend time with wise people so that I may become wise by learning from them. I know that You are my source of love, companionship and friendship. Help me to find Your love and friendship expressed through my relationship with members of the body of Christ.

Just as iron sharpens iron, so a friend sharpens a friend As we learn from each other, may we share the same love and have one mind and purpose. Help me, Lord, to be well-balanced in my friendships so that I will always please You rather than others.

Lord, I ask for divine connections and good friendships, and thank You for the courage and grace to let go of detrimental friendships. I ask for Your discernment for developing healthy relationships. Your Word says that two people are better than one because if one person falls, the other can reach out and help.

Father, only You know the hearts of people so help me to discern and not be deceived by outward appearances. Thank You, Lord, that every good and perfect gift comes from You and I thank You for quality friends.

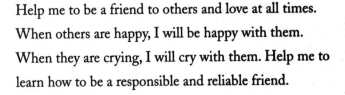

Help me to be a friend to others and love at all times. When others are happy, I will be happy with them. When they are crying, I will cry with them. Help me to learn how to be a responsible and reliable friend.

Develop in me, Lord, a fun personality and a good sense of humor. Help me to relax around people and to be myself – the person You created me to be. I want to be a faithful and trustworthy friend to the people You are sending into my life. You are my help, Father, in my friendships.

Jesus is my best friend. He is a real friend who is more loyal than a brother. He defined the standard when He said in John 15:13 that there is no greater love than to lay down one's life for his friends.

Thank You, Lord, that I can trust You with myself and my need for friends. I praise You that You are concerned with everything that concerns me. Hallelujah!

Scripture References

Proverbs 13:20 NIV	Proverbs 13:20 NIV
Ephesians 5:20 NIV	James 1:17 NIV
Philippians 2:2,3 NCV	Proverbs 17:17
1 Corinthians 15:33 WE	Romans 12:15 WE
Psalm 84:11 NIV	Proverbs 18:24 NLT

Ecclesiastes 4:9,10 NLT   Psalm 37:4,5 NCV

Proverbs 27:17 NLT

For Good Communication

Since I am Your child, Father, I am taught by You and You give me great peace. I will not copy the behaviors and customs of this world but I will let You transform me by changing the way that I think. Then, I will know Your will for me which is good and pleasing and perfect.

I will speak the truth in love and grow more like You every day. What I say will be important and right. I will always speak the truth, and make all my words honest and clear.

Father, give me an eagerness for Your laws rather than a love of money. I do not love the world or anything that comes from the world. Your love, Father, is in me. I am set free from my selfish desires and wanting everything I see. Because of You, I know the truth and that no lie comes from the truth.

I treasure Your wisdom, Lord, and will speak words of wisdom. I will pay close attention to Your words and will always keep them in mind. For they are the key to life for those who find them; they bring health to my whole body. I will be careful of what I think because my thoughts control my behavior.

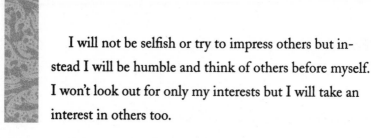

I will not be selfish or try to impress others but instead I will be humble and think of others before myself. I won't look out for only my interests but I will take an interest in others too.

In my life, I will think and act like You, Jesus. Amen.

Scripture References

Isaiah 54:13 NCV

Psalm 119:36 NLT

Romans 12:2 NLT

1 John 2:15,16,21 WE

Proverbs 4:8,20-23 NCV

Ephesians 4:15 NIV

Proverbs 8:6,8 NLT

Philippians 2:2-5 NLT

For Confidence in Relationships

Lord, You are my hope! I will always praise You. You alone are the source of my confidence, faith, hope, love, peace and forgiveness. I thank You for my family, church family and friends who are here to help me develop emotionally and spiritually. I am a friend of everyone who worships You and follows Your Word.

Father, You mean what You say and what You say goes. Your powerful Word is as sharp as a surgeon's scalpel, cutting through everything, whether doubt or defense, laying me open to listen and obey. I submit to You, Lord, and allow Your Word to shape my life so that I may identify and settle unresolved issues that have driven me to form unhealthy relationships in the past. I am focused on one thing: forgetting the past and looking forward to what lies ahead.

Jesus, I thank You that I have a full and true life in You and so I don't need to look to another person to bring me happiness and fulfillment because You make me so happy. I will not fall into the temptation to take responsibility for the behavior of others, and I will assume responsibility for my own actions.

Lord, You are my security and You will keep my foot from being caught in a trap. You have promised to never

leave or desert me. I am confident in my relationships because You are my Lord and Master. You have given me everything that I need to live a life that pleases You. All of this was given to me by Your own power. Hallelujah! I am a friend who loves all the time. I will continually think of others and with Your help, I will show them Your unconditional love.

In my relationships, I encourage love and worshipping together. We admit our faults to one another and pray for each other so that we may be healed. When a believing person prays, great things happen! My relationships are founded on love from a pure heart, a good conscience and a true faith in the name of Jesus. Amen.

Scripture References

Psalm 71:5 NCV	Proverbs 3:26 NLT
Psalm 92:4 MSG	Psalm 119:63 AMP
Hebrews 13:5 WE	1 Timothy 1:5 NCV
1 Corinthians 2:15,16 MSG	2 Peter 1:3,4 WE
Hebrews 4:12 MSG	Proverbs 17:17
Philippians 3: 13 NLT	Hebrews 10:24,25
Colossians 2:10 NCV	James 5:16 NCV

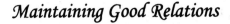

Maintaining Good Relations

Father, in the name of Jesus, I will not withhold good from those that deserve it when it is in my power to help them. I will give to everyone what I owe them. I will pay my taxes and government fees to those that collect them and I will give respect and honor to those who are in authority.

I will not become tired of helping others, for I will be rewarded when the time is right if I do not give up. So, right now, every time I get the chance, I will work for the benefit of all, starting with the people closest to me in the community of faith. Help me, Father, to be mindful to be a blessing to all those around me.

I will not pick a fight without reason, but will do my best to live at peace with everyone around me. Thank You, Father for Your help in living this way. In the name of Jesus. Amen.

<u>Scripture References</u>

Proverbs 3:27 NLT

Proverbs 3:30 NLT

Romans 13:7 NLT

Romans 12:18

Galatians 6:9,10 MSG

A Personal Prayer for Husbands

Father, in the beginning Your Word tells us that You provided a helper and companion for man. Now I have found a wife to be my companion and she is my treasure. I have received favor from the Lord. I won't ever forget kindness and truth. I will wear them like a necklace and write them on my heart as if on a tablet. Then, I will be respected and please both God and people.

I will say about my wife, "There are many capable women, but you surpass them all!" I will show her respect and praise her in public for all she does for me and our family. I will provide leadership to my wife the way Christ does to His Church, not by domineering but by cherishing. I will go all out in my love for her, exactly as Christ did for the Church – a love marked by giving, not getting.

It is my desire to give my wife what is due her, and I will purpose to share my personal rights with her. Father, I honor my wife and delight in her. In the new life of God's grace, we are equals. I will treat my wife as an equal so that our prayers are not hindered.

Lord, I love to worship You and obey Your teachings. My children will have great power in the land because

You bless them. Their houses will be full of wealth and riches and their goodness will continue forever. In the name of Jesus, amen.

Scripture References

Ephesians 5:22,23 MSG   Matthew 18:18

1 Corinthians 7:3-5 NCV   Genesis 2:18 MSG

Proverbs 18:22 NLT   1 Peter 3:7-9 NLT

Psalm 112:1-4 NCV   Proverbs 3:3,4 NCV

Proverbs 31:28-31 NLT

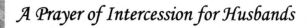

A Prayer of Intercession for Husbands

Father, in the name of Jesus, I take Your Word and declare this day that _____ listens to You and will live in peace, untroubled by fear of harm. _____ listens carefully to wisdom and sets his mind on understanding. He applies all of his power to the quest of it.

He lets kindness and truth always show like a necklace and writes them in his heart. He never walks away from wisdom for she guards his life. She will exalt and promote him and bring honor to him because he has embraced her. He can be sure that the Lord will keep him from harm.

When _____ walks, the Word and wisdom will guide him. They will guard him when he sleeps and speak to him when he is awake. He says only worthwhile and right things and every word is honest, not one is crooked or false.

_____ will live in a thoughtful way with me. He will treat me with honor and show me respect because God gives me the same blessing that he gives my husband - the grace that gives true life. He does this so that nothing will stop our prayers.

I say that the fruit of the righteous is a tree of life and the one who is wise saves lives. _____ and I choose to live this way because we love and respect each other.

Thank You, Father, that _____ is a man of good report – that he is successful in everything he sets his hand to. He is uncompromisingly righteous. He captures human lives for God as a fisher of men. As he does this he has the confidence that You are the Lord his God who teaches him what is good and leads him along the paths that he should follow. He has Your favor upon Him and Your will is done in his life!

Scripture References

Proverbs 1:33 NLT	Proverbs 6:22 NCV
Proverbs 2:2 NCV	Proverbs 8:6,8 NCV
Proverbs 3:3 NCV	1 Peter 3:7-9 NCV
Proverbs 4:8 MSG	Proverbs 11:30 NIV
Proverbs 3:26 NCV	Isaiah 48:17 NLT

Wives

In the name of Jesus, I will clothe myself with the beauty that comes from within, the unfading beauty of a gentle and quiet spirit, which is so precious to God. I choose to be a good, loyal wife to my husband and treat him with respect. By God's grace, I will be agreeable, sympathetic, loving, compassionate and humble. I will be a blessing and also receive blessings.

By Your Spirit, I am becoming more and more like You. Your bright glory is shining through me. You are creating a clean heart in me, Lord. I am an honest woman who is a crown for my husband. I will walk wisely and strengthen my family and not destroy them. Houses and wealth are inherited from parents but a wise wife is a gift from the Lord. Praise You, Lord, that You were so rich in kindness and grace that You purchased our freedom with the blood of Your Son and forgave our sins. You have showered Your kindness on us along with wisdom and understanding.

Holy Spirit, I ask You to help me understand and support my husband in ways that show my support for Christ. *Teach me to function so that I preserve my own personality while responding to his desires. We are one flesh, and I realize that this unity of persons that

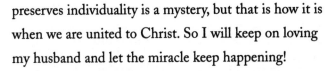

preserves individuality is a mystery, but that is how it is when we are united to Christ. So I will keep on loving my husband and let the miracle keep happening!

Just as my husband gives me all that he owes me, I seek to be fair and will give my husband all that I owe him as his wife.

I am strong and respected and joyful about my future. My words are wise and my advice is thoughtful. I watch over my family and am never lazy. Thank You Father that I have the wisdom that comes from You and it is pure, peaceful, gentle and easy to please. This wisdom is always ready to help those who are troubled and to do good for others. It is always fair and honest. Thank You Jesus for sharing that wonderful wisdom with me to be the best wife that I can possibly be! In Jesus' name. Amen.

Husbands, I encourage you to pray this prayer in third person for your wife.

**The Heart of Paul*, Ben Campbell Johnson. Copyright © 1976 by A Great Love, Inc., Toccoa, GA

Scripture References

Matthew 16:19 NKJV   Proverbs 19:14 NCV

Proverbs 14:1 NCV   Ephesians 1:7,8 NLT

Ephesians 5:22-23 MSG

2 Corinthians 3:18 NCV

1 Corinthians 7:2-5 NCV

Proverbs 12:4 NCV

1 Peter 3:1-5, 8, 9 NLT & MSG

Psalm 51:10 NKJV

Proverbs 11:6

Proverbs 31:25-27 NCV

James 3:17,18 NCV

Finding a Mate

Introduction

In our ministry we hear from many men and women who desire to be married. If that is your desire, we encourage you to ask the Lord to prepare you for marriage. Submit to God's future plans for your life, and purpose to please Him. Do not make your deliberations without knowing His will at the expense of your personal spiritual growth and transformation. Going from glory to glory (2 Corinthians 3:18) is not dependent on having a spouse.

Very often, each partner brings emotional baggage into the marriage relationship. As you prepare for marriage, remember that the anointing that was upon Jesus (Luke 4:18,19) is within you. This anointing will destroy every yoke of bondage (Isaiah 10:27) as God exposes emotional wounds and heals your brokenness.

Knowing the reality of your completeness in Christ Jesus will enable you to enter into a healthy relationship, one in which both you and your partner will grow together spiritually and in every other area of life. Seeking first the kingdom of God and His righteousness (Matthew 6:33), doing those things that are pleasing in

His sight (I John 3:22), will prepare you to be the person designed by Him to fulfill the role of husband or wife.

This prayer is written for your own growth and benefit.

Prayer

Father, I come to You in the name of Jesus, asking for Your will to be done in my life as I look to You for a marriage partner.

I ask that You prepare me for marriage by bringing my darkest secrets to light and revealing my motives. I submit to Your Word that exposes wounded emotions, walls of denial, emotional isolation, silence or excessive talking, anger, or rigidity or any wall that separates me from healthy relationships and from Your love and grace. The weapons that You have given me to bring my thoughts into agreement with Your Word are different from those that the world uses. These powerful weapons destroy the enemy's strong places.

I know the One in whom I trust and I am sure that He is able to guard what I have entrusted to him, whether I remain unmarried or married, until the day of His return.

Because I love You, Lord, I know that You are always at work for my good. Everything that happens to me fits

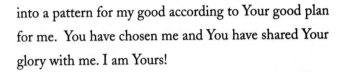

into a pattern for my good according to Your good plan for me. You have chosen me and You have shared Your glory with me. I am Yours!

I remove anything from my life that would get in the way of the race that is before me. I will never give up. But always look only to Jesus, the One who began our faith and who makes it perfect. You suffered death on the cross but accepted the shame because of the joy that God put before You. You are now on God's right side appealing to God for me!

I will run from the temptations that capture young people. With Your help I will follow what is right. I choose to be pure, loving, and easy to get along with. I will associate with people whose hearts are pure. I will stay away from stupid and senseless arguments that only lead to trouble. I will be kind to everyone, patient and gentle.

Father, more than anything else, I put Your work first and what You call good. Then, the other things will be mine as well. I won't worry about tomorrow. It will take care of itself.

I know that I can trust You because You loved me first. Even before You made the world, You loved us and chose us in Christ to be holy and without fault in Your

eyes. For in You, lives all the fullness of God in a human body so I am complete in my union with You.

I come before You, Father, expressing my desire for a Christian mate. I pray that Your will be done in my life. Now, I will enter into Your rest as I trust in You fully. Amen.

Scripture References

Matthew 6:10 NIV

Matthew 6:33-34 WE

1 Corinthians 4:5 NLT

1 John 4:19

2 Corinthians 10:4 NCV

Ephesians 1:4 NLT

2 Timothy 1:12 NLT

Colossians 2:9,10 NLT

Romans 8:28-30 NIV

Matthew 6:10 NIV

Hebrews 12:1-3 NCV

Hebrews 4:10

Romans 8:34 NCV

John 14:1

2 Timothy 2:22-25 WE

The Home

Father, I thank You that You have given me every spiritual blessing. I will build my home by wisdom and let good sense fill the rooms with priceless treasures. The house of the righteous has great treasure and it stands firm. My house brims with wealth and my generosity never runs dry in the name of Jesus.

My house is securely built on a solid rock. The flood-waters may come and try to rush against it but it will not shake. Jesus is my Cornerstone. Jesus is Lord over my household. My house will work willingly in whatever we do as though we were working for You, Lord, rather than for people. My family loves each other with the love of God and we live in peace. I entrust my home to Your protection and care.

Father, as for me and my family, we will serve the Lord in Jesus name. Hallelujah!

Scripture References

Ephesians 1:3 NCV	Acts 16:31
Proverbs 24:3,4 NLT	Philippians 2:10-11
Proverbs 15:6	Colossians 3:23 NLT
Proverbs 12:7	Colossians 3:14,15

Psalm 112:3 MSG

Luke 6:48 NLT

Acts 4:11

Acts 20:32

Joshua 24:15 NCV

PART IV:

PRAYERS FOR PARENTING

When Desiring to Have a Baby

Father, my spouse and I kneel in prayer to You. Our
Father, You are wonderful and glorious and all beings in
heaven and on earth were created by You. We pray that
we will become strong in You and thank You that You
live in our hearts because of our faith. We are deeply
rooted in Your love. Your love is too wonderful to be
measured, Lord. Because of Your love, our lives will be
filled with all that You are.

We praise You, Lord, because You give children to
the woman who has none and You make her a happy
mother. We thank You because You are the One who is
building our family. We receive Your gift of children for
they are a reward from You.

We thank You, Father, because we know that You
will give us what we ask for because we obey You and do
what pleases You.

Thank You that we will bear children as a vine bears
grapes and our household will be lush as a vineyard. The
children around our table will be as fresh and promising
as young olive shoots. We stand in awe of You, Lord.
Thank You for blessing those who fear You!

In Jesus' name we pray, amen.

Scripture References

Psalm 127:3 NLT   Psalm 113:9 NCV

1 John 3:22-23 WE   Psalm 128:3-4 MSG

Ephesians 3:14-19 NIV,NLT

For Pregnancy

Father, You know my heart and know that I have longed to be a mother, and now the miracle has happened! I am so thankful to You and I praise You knowing that my child's frame is not hidden from You. This baby is being shaped and formed in my womb by You, Lord. You know this baby inside and out. You know every bone in this body. Like an open book, You are watching my baby from conception until birth. All the days of my baby's life were all prepared even before he/she was conceived.

Thank You for this life that is developing within my body. I surround this baby with loving words day and night. You have filled my mouth with laughter and my heart with joy. I treasure every movement of life- the stretching of his/her limbs. I will choose to be full of joy because I know my moods affect this little one. Your praise is always on my lips and I will praise You at all times even when I don't feel like it.

Lord, You have blessed us and will continue to bless us all the days of our lives and we will live to enjoy our grandchildren. You are so wonderful to include us in Your plan of hope and success for this unborn child.

Scripture References

Psalm 103:14   Psalm 34:1 NCV

Psalm 139:13-16 MSG   Psalm 128:6

Psalm 16:7   Jeremiah 29:11

Philippians 4:4

Adopting a Child

Father, You alone know my heart and how I longed to conceive and bear my children. Forgive me when I blame You for not having this experience of having natural children. This has not been an easy cross to bear and has put stress on me and my family. But You, my Lord, by the power of Your word, have healed me and rescued me. Thank you, Lord for setting me free from my suffering and giving us a child after our own heart. People even say that he/she favors us.

Thank You that by Your power working in us, You can do much more than anything we can ask or imagine. Thank you for giving us the desire to adopt a child and for leading us to this special child that You had planned for us long ago. I ask You to help us train him/her in the right way so that when he/she is older they will not stray from it.

Prepare our hearts for the day that he/she understands about adoption; give us the right words to say and to let him/her know that he/she has always been loved and that this family chose him/her to be a part of us. Help us to show him/her that he/she is a precious member of our family and the one that God picked for us!

I ask You to help him/her know that he/she is like a letter written by You and delivered to us. But – not a letter written with pen and ink but written in our hearts by Your Spirit. (Child's name), God says that He has thoughts of good and not for disaster to give you a future and a hope. You are made in an amazing and wonderful way. He destined that we would be your father and mother. We know very well what God has done is wonderful!

Scripture References

Psalm 107:20 NIV

Luke 4:18 NIV

Ephesians 3:20 NCV

Psalm 37:4

Colossians 2:15

Ephesians 2:10 NLT

Proverbs 22:6 NCV

Ephesians 1:4

2 Corinthians 3:3 NIV

Jeremiah 29:11 NLT

Psalm 139:14 NCV

Blessing the Household

Father, as the head of this household, I declare and decree, "My family and I are going to worship and serve the Lord!"

All praise to You, the Father of our Lord Jesus Christ, who has blessed us with every spiritual blessing in the heavenly realms because we are united with Christ. We are led by the Spirit to worship You, Father, according to the truth. We know that You seek out those who want to worship You.

Lord, we acknowledge and welcome the presence of Your Holy Spirit here in our home. We thank You, Father, that Your Son, Jesus, is here with us because we have come together in His name, and the Holy Spirit is ever present with us.

Lord, Your divine power has given us everything we need to live and to serve You. We have these things because we know You and You called us by Your glory and goodness.

As spiritual leader of this home, I declare on the authority of Your Word that my family will be powerful in the land; my children will be honest people who will

be blessed. Their houses will be full of wealth and riches
and their goodness will continue forever.

In the name of Jesus I pray. Amen

Scripture References

Revelation 1:6

Joshua 24:15 NCV

Ephesians 1:3 NLT

John 4:23 NLT

Matthew 18:20

2 Peter 1:3 NCV

Psalm 112:2-3 NCV

Prayer of Blessing at the Table

This prayer was written for the head of the household
to pray not only to thank and praise God for His blessings, but also to cleanse and consecrate the food received
and to sanctify the family members who partake of it.
I encourage you to take your place as the head of your
household and bless the Father, who gives us our daily
bread.

Prayer

Father, thank You for giving us the food that we need
today. We receive this food with thanksgiving and praise,
for everything that You create is good. You bless our
bread and water and take sickness from us.

In the name of Jesus, we call this food clean and
thank You that it will only act as nourishment to our
bodies. Thank You for Your promise in Your Word that
even if we drink any deadly thing it will not hurt us for
the Holy Spirit that gives us live in Christ Jesus sets us
free from the law of sin and death.

In the name of Jesus, I pray. Amen.

Scripture References

Matthew 6:11 NLT   Mark 16:18

1 Timothy 4:4 NIV   Romans 8:2 NIV

Exodus 23:25

Parenting Skills

Father, I ask You to give me strength and wisdom for
the task of raising my children. I do not have the right
to claim that I have done anything on my own. You give
me the ability to do all that I do. Hallelujah! In every
situation help me to remember that Your grace is all suf-
ficient. Your power works best in my weakness.

Father, my children are prone to foolishness and fads.
I ask You for grace to apply the cure that comes through
tough-minded discipline. In the name of Jesus, I will
not make my children angry but will raise them with the
training and teaching of the Lord.

Thank you, Lord, that You have given me wise words
to speak so that I can teach my children to be kind. I
will teach them right from wrong so that when they are
grown they will still do right because they love You and
desire to please You. I will discipline my children with
love and resist the temptation to be domineering and
demanding.

Father, even when I am tired and worn out, my
children need me. I will watch over my children that You
have entrusted to me with a willing heart. I won't lord it
over my children but I will lead them by my own good

example. I will teach my children Your words over and over again. I will talk about Your commands all the time both at night and in the morning. Thank You for sending the Holy Spirit who is my Comforter, Strengthener, and Standby.

Real wisdom is Your wisdom. It is gentle and reasonable, overflowing with mercy and blessings, not hot one day and cold the next, not two-faced. I will remember that it is unwise to compare myself with my children or to compete with them. When I was a child, I spoke and thought and reasoned as a child. But when I grew up, I put away childish things. In the name of Jesus, I pull down every controlling, manipulative attitude. Instead, I will guide my children along the right paths for Your name's sake.

In the name of Jesus, I ask You to watch over Your words to make them true in my life. Amen.

Scripture References

Psalm 27:10	Philippians 2:4 AMP
2 Corinthians 3:5 WE	Deuteronomy 6:7 NIV
2 Corinthians 12:9 NLT	John 14:16 AMP
Proverbs 22:15 MSG	James 3:17 MSG
Ephesians 6:4 NCV	Colossians 1:13 MSG

Proverbs 31:26 NCV

Proverbs 22:6 NCV

Ephesians 6:1-4

Proverbs 13:24 MSG

1 Corinthians 13:11 NLT

Jeremiah 1:12 NCV

2 Corinthians 10:12

Peter 5:1-4 NLT

Psalm 23:3

To Parent with Confidence

Father, what an incredible job this is, raising these children in the training and instruction of the Lord. They are our future leaders whose lives will be a light for other people. Their lives will show good things and will praise You. Sometimes when we look with our natural eyes , situations in our nation seem hopeless. However, our hope is in the Lord. I will bless You, Lord. You guide me and even at night my heart instructs me. My heart is steady, God. I will sing and praise You, my God.

We will teach our children the right thing to do because we love You and belong to You, Lord. We will choose life and blessings so that our children might live! Lord, You are my hope and I have trusted You since I was young (since I confessed You as my Lord). Thank You, Father, that You have my children's lives all planned out. Plans to take care of them and not to abandon them, plans to give them a future that we hope for.

Hallelujah!

Scripture References

Ephesians 6:4 NIV   Psalm 108:1

Matthew 5:16 NCV   Genesis 1:26

Psalm 146:5   Ephesians 6:1-3

Deuteronomy 30:19 NLT   Zephaniah 3:5

Psalm 16:7 NLT   Psalm 71:5 NCV

Psalm 57:7 NCV   Jeremiah 29:11 MSG

To Parent with a Calm Spirit

Father, I know that losing my temper is not a fruit of the Spirit and so I am sorry, asking You and my children to forgive me for losing my temper. It says in Your Word that negative feelings and actions are selfish desires that my sinful self wants. So today I choose to be guided by Your Spirit so that I won't obey my selfish desires. Your Spirit makes me loving, happy, peaceful, patient, kind, gentle and self-controlled.

You are at work in me and helping me develop self-control. It says in Your Word that You didn't give me a spirit that makes me afraid but a spirit of power and love and self-control. Thank You for that promise!

As You work out Your plan in my life, I will rejoice because You have given me a peaceful heart which leads to a healthy life and body. A miserable heart means a miserable life so I choose to have a cheerful heart that fills the day with song.

I will choose to make my decisions calmly and patiently. My soft speech will break down resistance in my children. Thank You, Holy Spirit, for helping me to be self-controlled so that I might capture the heart and minds of my children.

When I am angry, I will not sin and I will not go to bed angry. Today, I will stop being bitter and angry and mad. I submit to Your Word that exposes unhealed hurts and unresolved anger from my past so I will be healed and ready to give my children a ready answer rather than reacting. I will not yell or be rude. Father, instead I choose to be kind and merciful and forgiving. I will raise my children with the training and teaching of You, Lord. A gentle answer will calm my children but an unkind answer will cause more anger.

Father, You know how I've always screamed when the children are fighting. I don't want to do this anymore! My great aim and quest in life is to live a life filled with love by following Your example. I don't want to discipline by heaping guilt and condemnation on them. Even though I feel like I am screaming louder to be heard, I am doing the very thing I tell them not to do. Help me to develop the fruit of the Spirit so that my life will be a demonstration of Your love.

The Proverbs 31 mother speaks only when she has something worthwhile to say and she always says it kindly. I don't want to just force my children to stop fighting but teach them how to resolve conflict. Show me a better way. You are my Teacher and I trust You to give me the wisdom that I need.

Help me to lead a life worthy of my calling because I have been called by You! I will strive to always be humble and gentle and patient with others. You chose me and You can be trusted to help and guide me in this awesome task! Your message works in me because I believe and I know You are working in me to help me want to do and be able to do what pleases You! Amen.

Scripture References

Galatians 5:13-26 WE

Ephesians 4:26

1 Thessalonians 5:24 NCV

Proverbs 14:30 NLT

Ephesians 4:31-32 NCV

Ephesians 4:1-3 NLT

Ephesians 6:4

1 Thessalonians 2:13 NCV

Ephesians 5:2 NLT

2 Timothy 1:7 NCV

Proverbs 31:26 MSG

James 1:5

Proverbs 15:15 MSG

Proverbs 15:1 NCV

Philippians 2:13 NCV

Train Them in the Way They Should Go

Father, forgive me for looking to my children for
fulfillment. They do bring me great joy but I have been
naïve in thinking that they would meet my needs. Forgive me for placing emotional demands on them when
You were present to give me everything I need through
Your wonderful riches in Christ Jesus. I am so grateful
and humbled that You chose me to be the mother of
these precious ones. Forgive me for those times when I
don't enjoy being a mother or when I blame my children
for my behavior. Help me to make an attitude adjust-
ment. Thank You, Holy Spirit, for reminding me to cast
down my negative thoughts and thank You for making
me Your masterpiece. You created me anew in Jesus so
that I can do the good things that You planned for me
long ago.

You are my God. I can't get enough of You. In my
heart I long for You. Help me to quiet the distractions
so that I may hear Your voice. You have called me to be a
minister to Your precious ones and now You are teaching
me to direct them on the right path so that when they
are older, they will not leave it. Help me to teach them
how to make decisions that are in line with Your plans
for them. Plans to take care of them, not abandon them
and plans to give them a future that they hope for.

How precious are your thoughts about me, O God.
They cannot be numbered. I can't even count them; they
outnumber the grains of sand. You knew my children before the world was made and You are always with them.
You will never leave them or forsake them!

Father, thank You that You are helping me to teach
and train my children in Your Word and teaching them
Your ways so that they can live successfully, fulfilling
their destinies. Holy Spirit, I ask You to help me mold
their thoughts so they will resist the enemy's attempt to
lie to them. They will make wise decisions even when
I'm not with them.

Thank You for giving my children the courage to
stand as bright shining lights in a dark and perverse
world. I say that my children will be world-changers.
Others will see their light shine and give glory to You.

Scripture References

Philippians 4:19 NCV	Psalm 139:17-18 NLT
Ephesians 2:10 NLT	Ephesians 1:4 NCV
Psalm 63:1 MSG, NCV	Hebrews 13:5
Proverbs 22:6 NLT	James 4:7
Jeremiah 29:11 MSG	Matthew 5:14, 16

To Know God's Will

Father, in Jesus' name, I thank You that You are guiding me along the best pathway for my life and advising me and watching over me. I thank You that I am Your child and you sent Jesus to save me and make me wise, holy, and right with God. Thank You that I do hear Your voice. You are the Good Shepherd and I won't run from You because I know Your voice. You give me new strength and lead me on paths that are right for the good of Your name.

Thank You, Father, that my lifestyle is like sunlight at dawn that keeps getting brighter and brighter. As I follow You, Lord, I believe that my life shines brighter and becomes clearer each day.

I praise You that Jesus was made unto me wisdom. You make Your will for me clear and lead me in a plain pathway. I trust in You with all my heart and not my own understanding. I will always seek Your will and You will show me which path to take. I believe that as I trust in You completely, that You will show me the way of life. Amen.

Scripture References

Psalm 32:8 NLT

John 10:2-5, 11, 14 NLT

Psalm 23:3 NCV

Proverbs 4:18 NCV

1 Corinthians 1:30 NLT

1 Corinthians 14:33

Proverbs 3:5,6 NLT

Psalm 16:11 NLT

When You Feel Like Giving Up

Father, thank You that I can ask You for help! Being a parent is the most difficult job I have tried to do. Today I am tired and am carrying heavy loads. I come to You, Lord Jesus, to learn Your teachings and find rest for my life. Your burden is easy and Your load light. I want to know You and to know Your truth. I desire with all my heart to bring up my children with the discipline and instruction that comes from You, Lord. Nothing will bring me greater happiness than to hear that my children are living in the right way.

My children were created by You and they exist because You created what You pleased. It overwhelms me when I think about You entrusting them to my care. They could have been born in any time period but You chose me to conceive and birth them. I may have made my own plans in my mind but You determine my steps, Father.

Thank You for loving me enough to set me on the path that You ordained for me before the beginning of time. Thank You for my wonderful children that You have given to me. I would never have known You as I do today if these precious ones were not a valuable part of my life. Thank You, Father, for being the Keeper and Protector of my children. In the name of Jesus. Amen.

Scripture References

Matthew 11:28-30 NCV   Daniel 2:21

Ephesians 6:4 NLT   Proverbs 16:9 NLT

3 John 1:4 WE   Ephesians 1:4

Revelation 4:11 NLT   Romans 8:28

Colossians 1:16   Genesis 14:22

Ephesians 2:10 NLT   Psalm 91:1-2

PART V:

PRAYERS FOR CHILDREN AND GRANDCHILDREN

Salvation of Grandchildren

Father, I come before You with the names of my children and their children upon my heart as a continual reminder before You. I ask You, Lord, to raise up and send the perfect person to each one to share the gospel message in a way that they will hear and understand. Father, Thank You for preparing their hearts and bringing them to repentance by Your kindness and love. My children will not be able to resist the sweet drawing of the Holy Spirit.

Your Spirit is here to show the people of this world the truth about sin and God's righteousness and the coming judgment. Father, by Your Spirit You will reveal to them that Jesus is the Son of God just as You did to Peter in Matthew 16.

Father, I use Your weapons that You have provided to me to knock down the enemy's strongholds that would try to keep my children from hearing and understanding the truth. In the name of Jesus, I break down strongholds and thoughts that would keep them from knowing You.

My children and grandchildren will call upon You and be saved! They will confess that You are Lord and

they will turn from darkness to light. By faith, I thank You now for their salvation and redemption. Jesus is Lord over my family!

Scripture References

Exodus 28:29 NCV

2 Corinthians 5:19

Romans 10:9,10

John 16:8,9 NLT

1 John 1:9

Romans 5:8

2 Corinthians 5:17

John 14:6

John 3:16

Romans 10:13

John 6:37 NIV

Ephesians 2:1-10 NCV

John 10:10

John 1:12

Romans 3:23

2 Corinthians 5:21

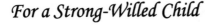

For a Strong-Willed Child

Father, thank You that I can come to you to vent and bring my frustrations to You. I find it difficult to help my children with their schoolwork and relationships. I know sometimes they feel so unloved and alone. It hurts my heart when I don't know how to convince them that You have made them in an amazing and wonderful way. Give _____(name of child or names of children) revelation of Your unconditional love for them. They love Your Word and Your promises even at an early age.

I know in my heart that You loved my children from long ago and chose them to be voices of hope to their generation. I ask You to help me overcome my feeling of hopelessness as I try to reach them. Forgive me for the mistakes that I have made and tell me what to say and show me what to do. I desire to love them with the love You have placed in my heart by Your Spirit, Father.

Even though they may struggle with perfectionism, help me to teach them that You are greater than any mistakes they make and how to use their failures as stepping stones. You are preparing them for the good things that You have planned for them to do. Your kindness and love will always be with them each day of their lives.

I declare that _____(name of child or names of children) will fulfill their divine destiny and win many people for You! Amen.

Scripture References

Psalm 139:14 NCV

Psalm 119:140

Jeremiah 31:3

Ephesians 1:4 WE

Psalm 25:4 NCV

Philippians 4:13

Romans 8:28

Ephesians 2:10

Psalm 23:6

To Know Who They Are in Christ

Father, in the name of Jesus I speak over my children that they have the mind of Christ. Teach them to understand what Christ is thinking! I thank You, Lord, that they are set free by Your blood and they have forgiveness of sins and they know the richness of Your grace.

I pray for them, asking You to give them wisdom and eyes to see clearly and to understand all You have done for them. May Your bright light make their way plain so that they will know what pleases You and give them the courage to do Your will.

May they always live in fellowship with You, for they are Your children in Christ Jesus. They can do everything through You because You give them strength.

Open their eyes that they may understand that they have been made the righteousness of God in Christ Jesus and that they are brand new creations in You. The past is forgotten and everything is new. You have chosen them and they are accepted. They are light in a dark world and completely victorious through You.

Thank You, Father, for loving them and giving to them everything that they need in this life.

<u>Scripture References</u>

2 Corinthians 5:17 NLT   Romans 8:1

Romans 6:11   Galatians 3:26

1 Corinthians 1:30 NLT   Ephesians 1

Ephesians 5:8 MSG   Romans 8:37 NCV

1 Corinthians 2:16 NLT   Philippians 4:13 NLT

To Understand Their Value

Introduction

It is vital that your children see themselves as valuable and precious. They face pressures that we can't imagine. Recently I was talking with a group of young people, and they expressed the pressure of having to get into the "rat race" at an early age. They felt driven to be successful and felt inferior if they did not live up to the expectations of others.

Talk with your children, write notes or e-mails, send texts affirming them, and validate their feelings. With prayer as your foundation, you can be an instrument of encouragement, a place of safety for them. You can help launch your children (and grandchildren) into their destinies.

Help your children accept themselves as God made them for His purposes. In his book *Your Best Life Now*, Joel Osteen writes:

A Word of Wisdom: *It is vital that you accept yourself and learn to be happy with who God made you to be. If you want to truly enjoy your life, you must be at peace with yourself. Many people constantly feel badly about*

themselves. They are overly critical of themselves, living with all sorts of self-imposed guilt and condemnation. No wonder they're not happy; they have a war going on inside. They're not at peace with themselves. And if you can't get along with yourself, you will never get along with other people. The place to start is by being happy with who God made you to be.

Prayer

Father, I come before Your throne where I can receive mercy and grace to help my children, _____ (name them) when they need it.

I receive and welcome these children as gifts from You. They are my reward and I will pray for them and not give up! I will love them unconditionally and build them up, affirming their strengths. Give me wisdom to hear beyond their words and to help them explore how they can overcome their weaknesses. Father, thank You for the Holy Spirit who gives them encouragement and shows them their value.

Open their eyes and show them that You are merciful and it is Your wonderful kindness that saves them. You raised them from death to life with Christ Jesus and You have given them a place with Christ in heaven.

You chose my children before the foundation of the world. You made them who they are and they are Your design. Because You are our God, You will guard them as You would guard Your own eyes. You will hide them in the shadow of Your wings. Hallelujah!

Scripture References

Hebrews 4:16 NCV

Ephesians 2:4-6 WE

John 15:16

Psalm 17:8 NLT

Psalm 127:3 NLT

Ephesians 1:4

Ephesians 2:10

For Your Children's Future

Father, Your Word tells me that children are a gift
and reward from You. You promise that they will have
much peace when taught in Your ways. I dedicate _____
_____ to You today, that they may be raised
as You desire and will follow the path that You choose
for them. Father, I speak Your Word this day over them.
I thank You that when we speak Your words out, they
don't return to You without doing everything that You
send them to do.

Heavenly Father, I commit myself, as a parent to
teach_____to live the right way, trusting in
Your promise that when they are grown they will still do
right. I give all my worries of raising my children to You,
Lord, knowing that You care for me. I will not provoke
my children but I will love them and leave them in Your
care. I will do as Your Word tells me to and teach my
children Your commands. I will talk about them when
we are sitting at home, on the road, when we lie down
and when we get up. Your grace is all that I need. Your
power works best where I am weak.

My children obey and honor both their parents,
which is the first commandment with a promise. They

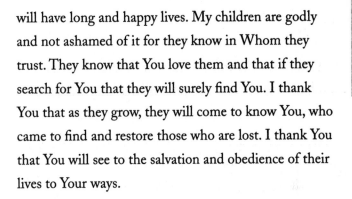

will have long and happy lives. My children are godly and not ashamed of it for they know in Whom they trust. They know that You love them and that if they search for You that they will surely find You. I thank You that as they grow, they will come to know You, who came to find and restore those who are lost. I thank You that You will see to the salvation and obedience of their lives to Your ways.

Heavenly Father, I thank You now that You will send workers across my children's paths to show them the way of salvation through Your Son, Jesus. I am thankful that we will be able to be aware of Satan's schemes and escape from his trap. You have given my children the grace and strength to walk through the gate to life.

I pray that even as Jesus became wise and grew strong, so my children will be blessed with the same wisdom and that You will pour out Your favor and blessings on them.

I praise You in advance for my children's future spouses. You desire my children to be holy and make wise decisions concerning their bodies during their dating years. I speak blessings to the future marriage of each of my children, and believe that they will have godly households, letting the love and faith of Christ Jesus be their model. Continue to prepare them to be the men and women of God that You desire them to be.

My children will be diligent and hard-working. You promise great blessings to them and they will always have more than enough. Serving You helps them in every way by bringing blessings in this life and in the future life, too.

Father, thank You for protecting my children and being their place of safety. I trust in You for all of this.

In Jesus' name I pray. Amen.

Scripture References

Psalm 127:3 NLT	Matthew 7:14 NLT
Isaiah 54:13 NCV	Luke 2:52
Isaiah 55:11 MSG	Hebrews 13:4
1 Thessalonians 4:3 WE	Proverbs 22:6 NCV
1 Peter 5:7 NCV	Ephesians 5:22-25
Ephesians 6:4	2 Timothy 1:13 NLT
Deuteronomy 6:7 NCV	Proverbs 13:11
2 Corinthians 12:9 NLT	Proverbs 20:13 NCV
Ephesians 6:1-3 NLT	Romans 12:11
2 Timothy 1:12	1 Timothy 4:8 NCV
Proverbs 8: 17,32 NLT	Psalm 91:1,11 NLT
Luke 19:10 MSG	2 Corinthians 2:11
Matthew 9:38	2 Timothy 2:26 NLT
Job 22:30	

Wise Choice of Friends

Father, I come boldly to Your throne where I will receive Your mercy and find grace to help me when I need it the most! I ask You to help my children meet new friends. I know that You are the source of love and friendship. Every good action and every perfect gift is from You, God. You never deny us any good thing so I am convinced that it is Your will for my children to have godly friendships.

Your Word reveals the purpose and value of healthy friendships. Holy Spirit, I ask You to teach my children what they need to know to be a good friend. Help them to be friendly and love at all times. Help them to live in peace with everyone as much as possible.

I pray that when they and their friends come together, that they will encourage each other and build each other up instead of bringing each other down. Help them not to play favorites but to honor You by accepting each other just as You accepted them.

Help them to be kind and loving to each other and to forgive each other just as You forgave them in Christ. I pray that they get along with each other and learn to be considerate of one another, cultivating a life in common.

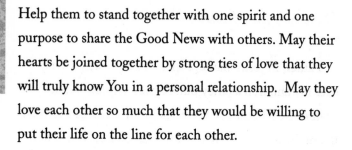

Help them to stand together with one spirit and one purpose to share the Good News with others. May their hearts be joined together by strong ties of love that they will truly know You in a personal relationship. May they love each other so much that they would be willing to put their life on the line for each other.

I thank You, Father, for my children's new friends. In Jesus' name I pray, amen.

Scripture References

Hebrews 4:16 NLT

James 1:17 NCV

Psalm 84:11 NLT

1 Corinthians 1:10 MSG

Proverbs 13:20

Proverbs 18:24

Proverbs 17:17 NCV

Romans 12:18 NIV

James 2:1 NLT

Romans 15:7 NLT

Ephesians 4:2,32 NCV

Ecclesiastes 4:9,10

Philippians 1:27 NLT

Philippians 2:2

Colossians 2:2 NLT

John 15:13 MSG

Children at School

Father, in Jesus' name, I speak Your Word this day over my children as they pursue their education and training at school. You are working in them, giving them the desire and the power to do what pleases You. They will always be on the top and never at the bottom.

You will cause my children to be respected and to be pleasing to both You and to their teachers and classmates. I ask You to give them wisdom so they can be capable of learning and understanding in all their subjects.

Thank You for giving _____ (name your children) an appreciation for education, help them understand that the source of all knowledge is in You. You are creating in them an appetite for education and a desire to learn and know more. You will guide them as they learn, grow and achieve. I pray that they will be diligent in all their ways. I pray for my children, asking that they be made wise and understand what it means to truly know You.

Father, I thank You that my children have protection because they stay in Your shadow. You are their fortress and their place of safety and they can always trust in You. My children will know mercy, grace and truth and will

stand rooted and grounded in Your love. They will not be influenced by every new teaching and they will not fall into the tricks of following the wrong path.

Thank You for the angels that protect my children wherever they go. They don't have to be afraid of anything because evil will not touch them or conquer them. You rescue them from every trap! Thank You that they are confident and fearless and can face their foes triumphantly.

I pray that my children's teachers will be godly men and women of integrity. Give their teachers understanding hearts and wisdom to walk in the ways of virtue. In Jesus' name. Amen.

Scripture References

Philippians 2:13 NLT	Psalm 91:1,2 NCV,NIV
Deuteronomy 28:1,2,13 NLT	Ephesians 4:14 NCV
Proverbs 3:4 NCV	Psalm 91:3-11 NLT
1 Kings 4:29	Ephesians 1:17 NCV
Daniel 1:4	Psalm 112:8 NLT

Safety

Father, in the name of Jesus, I lift myself and my family up to You and pray a wall of protection around us – our home and property. I thank You, Father, that You are a wall of fire around us and that Your angels protect us.

I thank You that we live under the protection of God Most High and we stay in the shadow of God Almighty. We will say to You, Lord, that You are our place of safety and protection. You are our God and we trust You! You will cover us with Your feathers and hide us under Your wings. We will not fear any danger by night or an arrow during the day. We will only watch and see the wicked punished.

You are our fortress and we run to You for safety. Because of this, no terrible disasters will strike us or our home. You will command Your angels to protects us wherever we go. You have said in Your Word that You will save whoever loves You. You will protect those who know You. You will be with us in trouble, You will rescue us and honor us and give us a long, full life and show us Your salvation. Not a hair of our head will perish.

Thank You, Father for your watch, care, and protection over my family and me. In Jesus' name. Amen.

Scripture References

Job 1:10 NLT

Zechariah 2:5

Psalm 34:7 NIV

Psalm 91:1,2 NCV

Psalm 91:4,5 NCV

Psalm 91:8 NCV

Psalm 9:9-11 NCV

Psalm 91:14-16 NCV

Luke 21:18 NIV

Peaceful Sleep

Introduction

I know that when your children are young, especially babies, that sleep can be very inconsistent and the nights exhausting. I want to encourage you to pray this prayer over your child. Although their sleep might not become consistent for months and sometimes years, remember that this is just a season and "this too shall pass." Our firstborn slept all night for the first time when he was eighteen months old, but we made it. Our second child slept all night from the time we brought her home from the hospital, for which I was very grateful, but this is unusual. The two younger children followed the "norm" sleeping all night after a period of time. Praise God that He made a way for us. Christ Jesus gives you the strength to face anything (Philippians 4:13).

Prayer:

Father, thank You for peaceful sleep and for Your angels that surround us. Praise the Lord for angels that are mighty and carry out Your plans. They listen for Your instructions and obey Your voice. You command Your angels to protect us wherever we go.

We capture every thought and make it give up and obey You, Father. I thank You that Your Word says that we can go to bed without fear and we can lie down and sleep soundly. Praise You, Lord, for being our guide. Even in the darkest night, Your teachings instruct us. We will always look to You as You are always with us. With all of our hearts, we will celebrate that we can safely rest. You give sleep to those who are Your children. Thank You, Father, that we can sleep soundly because You keep us safe!

Scripture References

Psalm 34:7 NLT   Proverbs 3:24 NLT

Psalm 103:20 NCV & NLT   Psalm 16:7-9 NLT

Psalm 91:11 NLT   Psalm 127:2 NCV

2 Corinthians 10:5 NCV   Psalm 4:8

Children with Special Needs

Father, I approach the throne of grace with confidence, so that I may receive mercy and find grace to help us in our time of need. You are the God of miracles and You have performed true miracles throughout history. I pray as Hannah of the Old Testament, asking for Your grace to be manifested in this special child You have entrusted to us.

I pray for my child who has special needs, asking You to make him/her wise and help him/her understand what it means to know You, our Father-God. May light flood his/her heart and may he/she understand the hope that was given when You chose this child who is a gift to us from You. Thank You for this child who is a blessing to us. I ask You to give peace to my child that passes all understanding. I pray for my child to be healthy, for this precious one to be saved and filled with Your Spirit, and for the fruit and gifts of the Spirit to be present in him/her.

I pray that this child will always put hope in You so that he/she will have no reason to be discouraged or sad. For You, O Lord, are a shield around _____ and the One who holds his/her head high. Your joy makes my child strong!

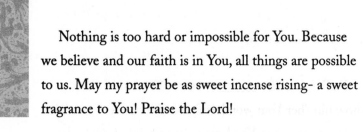

Nothing is too hard or impossible for You. Because we believe and our faith is in You, all things are possible to us. May my prayer be as sweet incense rising- a sweet fragrance to You! Praise the Lord!

In the name of Jesus I pray. Amen.

Scripture References

Hebrews 4:16 NIV

Jeremiah 1:12 NCV

Ephesians 1:17,18 NLT

Psalm 119:89

Luke 1:37

Mark 9:23 NCV

Psalm 141:2 AMP & MSG

Psalm 145:14

Psalm 3:3

Nehemiah 8:10 NCV

Ephesians 2:10

2 Corinthians 1:3

1 Thessalonians 5:23

Psalm 42:22 NCV

For Adult Children

Father, I bring _____ before You, asking You to show him/her Your wonderful plan for his/her life; make it clear to him/her. You have rescued him/her from the dark power of Satan and brought _____ into the kingdom of Your dear Son, Jesus. Father, give him/her spiritual wisdom and insight so that he/she may grow in You and understand the confident hope that You have given to those You called.

_____ made some decisions that could have destroyed him/her, but You remain faithful even when we are unfaithful. Thank You that You will rebuild and restore the wasted years and all the heartaches. You are the One who saves, forgives and only You will satisfy _____. As he/she stands now at a crossroads, may he/she hear and know Your voice. Open his/her eyes that he/she might see and choose life. Thank You for hearing and answering my prayer in the name of Jesus.

<u>Scripture References</u>

Jeremiah 29:11	Jeremiah 30:17
Colossians 1:9, 13 NCV	Psalm 103:2-5 NCV
Ephesians 1:17-19 NLT	John 10:4-5

2 Timothy 2:13 NLT   John 11:41

Isaiah 58:12 NCV

PART VI:

PERSONAL
PRAYERS

To Walk in Faith and Power

Father, I thank You that my children have power because the Holy Spirit has come upon them and they will
tell everyone about You all over the world!

In the name of Jesus, I have not stopped giving
thanks to You for _____(names of
children). I always remember them in my prayers, asking
that You give them a spirit of wisdom and revelation to
know You better. May they know that Your power is very
great for all of us who believe and that power is the same
as the great strength God used to raise Christ from the
dead.

Father, thank You for giving to each of my children a
measure of faith. It is by Your grace that they have been
saved through faith and they live by the faith of the Son
of God who treats us with great mercy. You love them
and gave Your life for them. They are strong in You,
Lord, and in Your mighty power.

I pray that from Your glorious and unlimited resources that You will empower them with inner strength
through Your Spirit that they may know how wide, how
long, how high and how deep Your love is. May they be
made complete with all the fullness of life and power
that comes from You.

All glory to You, God who is able through Your mighty power to accomplish infinitely more than we might ask or think. Amen!

Scripture References

Ephesians 1:16-20 NCV

Romans 12:3

Galatians 2:20 NLT

Ephesians 3:16-20 NLT

Acts 1:8 WE

Ephesians 2:8

Ephesians 6:10 NIV

Abiding in Jesus

Lord, I am sticking with Your Word and living out what You tell me. It is my desire to be a true disciple of Yours! I will stay joined to You so that You will stay joined to me. Just as a branch cannot produce fruit unless it stays joined to the vine, I cannot produce fruit unless I stay joined to You.

Lord, because You are the Vine and I am a branch joined to You, I will produce lots of fruit. Because I remain joined to You, Your words become part of me. I can ask for anything and it will be granted!

When I produce much fruit, it brings great glory to You. By Your grace, I will show and prove myself to be a true follower of Your Son, Jesus. He has loved me even as You, Father, have loved Him. I am remaining in Your love.

Lord, when I obey Your commandments, I remain in Your love just as Jesus obeyed your commandments and remained in Your love. You have told me all these things so that I will be filled with joy. Your joy will overflow! Your commandment is to love each other in the same way that You have loved us.

Father, thank You for Your Word - it is the truth that makes me free. I am part of You, Lord, and those who are Yours do not continue sinning because the new life from God remains in them. They have become children of God. Praise You, Father! I have taken Your Word to heart and it keeps me from sinning against You. Christ lives in my heart because of my faith. I will stand firm and be deeply rooted in Your love and how wide and long and high and deep that love is.

I pray that I may know all about Your love, although it is too wonderful to measure. Then, my life will be filled with Your fullness. Your power at work in me can do far more than I dare ask or imagine. Amen.

Scripture References

John 8:31 MSG

John 15:4,5 MSG

John 15:7-12 NLT

John 8:32

Ephesians 3:19-21 NCV

1 John 3:9 NCV

Psalm 119:11 NCV

Ephesians 3:17,18 WE

John 17:17

To Pray

Father, in the name of Jesus, I thank You for calling me to be a fellow worker in Your field. I will always pray and never lose hope.

Jesus, You are the Son of God and I will never stop trusting You. You help me in my weaknesses. There are times that I do not know how to pray as I should. But Your Spirit prays for me with deep feelings that words cannot explain. You see what is in my heart and Your Spirit prays for me in harmony with Your own will. This is why I can be so sure that every detail in my life is worked into something good.

I will not worry about anything but will pray and ask You for everything that I need, always giving thanks. I believe that I have received the things that I ask for in prayer because You will give them to me.

God made him (Jesus) who had no sin to be sin for us, so that in Him we might become the righteousness of God. Thank You that we have "right standing" with You, Father. When I pray, You hear and answer prayer so that You are glorified. I will produce much fruit and show that I am Your follower and this will bring glory to You. Amen.

Scripture References

1 Corinthians 3:9 NLT	Mark 11:24 NCV
Luke 18:1 NCV	2 Corinthians 5:21 NIV
James 5:16b NCV	Romans 8:28 MSG
John 15:7,8 NCV	Philippians 4:6 NCV
Romans 8:26,27 NLT	

To Trust in the Lord

Father, You are my God. I worship You with all my
heart. I long for You just as I would long for a stream
in a scorching desert. I know that You hear Your people
when they call to You for help. You rescue them from all
their troubles. Many are against me, but You keep me
safe in the battle. You give me the victory! I depend on
You and I have chosen to trust You since I believed. I can
be sure that You will keep me safe. In Christ, I have been
made right with God and my prayers have great power
and produce wonderful results!

Jesus is the high priest of my faith. I am completely
free to enter the Most Holy Place without fear because
of the blood of the Lamb. I can enter through a new and
living way that Jesus opened for me. I am confident that
You hear me whenever I ask for anything that pleases
You. And since I know that You hear me when I make
my requests, I also know that You will give me what I
ask for.

In the moment that I get tired in the waiting, Your
Spirit is right alongside helping me along. If I don't
know how or what to pray, Your Spirit helps me pray,
making prayer out of my wordless sighs and my aching

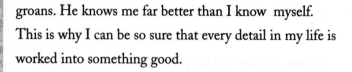

groans. He knows me far better than I know myself.
This is why I can be so sure that every detail in my life is
worked into something good.

In the name of Jesus, I will keep on believing God.
I know it will bring me great rewards. I will learn to be
patient and believe so that I will please You, Lord, and
receive what You have promised. I live by faith in the
Son of God who loved me and gave himself to save me.
Hallelujah! Praise You Lord!

Scripture References

Psalm 63:1 NLT   Hebrews 3:1 NCV

Hebrews 10:19-25 NCV   Psalm 34:17 NLT

Psalm 55:17,18 NCV   1 John 5:14,15 NLT

Proverbs 3:26 NCV   Romans 8:26-28 MSG

1 Corinthians 1:30 NCV   Psalm 71:5 NLT

Hebrews 10:35,36 WE   James 5:16 NLT

Galatians 2:20 NCV

Receiving a Discerning Heart

Father, I thank You for giving me an understanding heart so that I can know the difference between right and wrong.

I pray that my love will grow more and more and that I will fully know and understand how to make the right choices so that I will still be pure and without wrong when Christ returns. You will fill me with good things in my life that bring glory and praise to You!

Father, I will trust in You with all my heart and I will not depend on my own understanding. Your commandments give me understanding so no wonder I hate every false way of life. Your Word is a lamp to guide my feet and a light for my path.

Joseph, in Genesis 41:39-41 NIV, was described as a discerning and wise man who was put in charge of the entire land of Egypt. As You were with Joseph, so will You be with me. You will cause me to find favor at my place of employment, at home, or wherever I may be.

I pray that I will have great wisdom and understanding in spiritual things and use common sense in my decisions so that I will live the kind of life that honors

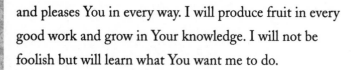

and pleases You in every way. I will produce fruit in every good work and grow in Your knowledge. I will not be foolish but will learn what You want me to do.

In the name of Jesus I pray, amen.

Scripture References

1 Kings 3:9 NLT

Proverbs 3:1-4

Philippians 1:9-11 NCV

Colossians 1:9,10 NCV

Proverbs 3:5 NLT

Joshua 1:5

Genesis 41:39-41 NIV

Ephesians 5:17 NCV

Psalm 119:104,105 NLT

Letting Go of Bitterness

Introduction

In interviews with divorced men and women, I have been encouraged to write a prayer on overcoming bitterness.

Often the injustice of the situation in which these people find themselves creates deep hurts, wounds in the spirit, and anger that is so near the surface that the individuals involved risk sinking into the trap of bitterness and revenge. Their thoughts may turn inward as they consider the unfairness of the situation and dwell on how badly they have been treated. Also, those who suffer abandonment by their parent(s) often harbor bitterness.

In a family divorce situation, bitterness sometimes distorts ideas of what is best for the child/children involved. One parent (and sometimes both parents) will use the child/children against the other. Unresolved anger often moves one marriage partner to hurt the one he or she holds responsible for the hurt and sense of betrayal which they feel.

There is healing available. There is a way of escape for all who will turn to the Healer, obeying Him and trusting Him.

Prayer

Father, life seems so unjust, so unfair. The pain of rejection is almost more than I can bear. My past relationships have ended in strife, anger, rejection and separation.

Lord, help me to not be bitter or angry or mad. Help me to never shout or say things to hurt others.

You are the one who has come to free those who have been treated unfairly. I receive emotional healing by faith, and I thank You for giving me the grace to stand firm until the process is complete.

Thank You for wise counselors. Thank You for Your Holy Spirit, my Counselor, who comes to show me what is true. Thank You for helping me to work out with fear and trembling to show the results of my salvation. You are working in me giving me the desire and power to do what pleases You.

In the name of Jesus, I choose to forgive those who have wronged me. I choose to live a life of forgiveness because You have forgiven me. With the help of the Holy Spirit, I will get rid of all bitterness, rage, anger, harsh words, and slander. I want to be kind to others, tenderhearted and forgiving.

With the help of the Holy Spirit, I will work at living in peace with everyone and work at living a holy life. I will protect others so that none of us fails to receive the grace of God. I will watch out that no poisonous root of bitterness grows up to trouble me.

I will watch and pray that I don't enter into temptation or cause others to stumble.

Thank You, Father, that whom the Son makes free is truly free. I have defeated bitterness and resentment by the blood of the Lamb and Your message.

In Jesus's name. Amen.

Scripture References

Ephesians 4:31 NCV   Ephesians 4:31,32 NLT

Luke 4:18 NCV   Hebrews 12:14,15 NLT

Isaiah 10:27   Matthew 26:41

Proverbs 11:14   Romans 14:21

John 15:26 NCV   Jeremiah 1:12 NCV

Philippians 2:12,13 NLT   John 8:36 NCV

Matthew 5:44   Revelation 12:11 NLT

To Be Well-Balanced

Father, in the name of Jesus, I approach Your throne of grace with confidence so that I may receive mercy and find grace to help me in my time of need.

Forgive me for getting caught up in my own pride. Sometimes I behave as though I am indispensable at home, at the office, at church, and in other situations. I become irritable and fatigued, feeling that no one appreciates all that I do. Help me to step back and take a long look at myself. Your light penetrates my human spirit, exposing every hidden motive and wrong attitude.

Jesus said, "Come to me, all of you who are tired and have heavy loads, and I will give you rest. Accept my teachings and learn from me, because I am gentle and humble in spirit, and you will find rest for your lives. The burden that I ask you to accept is easy; the load I give you to carry is light" (Matthew 11:28-30 NCV).

Everything on earth has its own time and its own special season. Help me to keep my priorities in order and stay focused. With Your help, I choose to fulfill my call and responsibilities whether at home or at the workplace. Also help me to take time to find rest for my soul as well as have fun!

I give all my worries to You because I know that You care for me. I will stay well-balanced, self-controlled and alert. The devil prowls around like a roaring lion looking for someone to devour. I resist him, standing firm in the faith, because I know that my brothers throughout the world are undergoing the same kinds of pressure.

In Your kindness You called me to share in Your eternal glory by means of Christ Jesus. So after I have suffered a little while, You will restore, support, and strengthen me, and You will place me on a firm foundation.

All power and glory to You forever! Amen.

Scripture References

Hebrews 4:16 NIV	Ecclesiastes 3:1 NCV
Proverbs 20:27 NLT	Matthew 11:29
2 Corinthians 6:14 NLT	1 Peter 5:7-11 NLT

To Receive Jesus as Savior and Lord

Father, it is written in Your Word that if I declare with my mouth, "Jesus is Lord" and if I believe in my heart that You raised Him from the dead, then I will be saved. So, I declare with my mouth that Jesus is my Lord. I make Him Lord of my life right now. I believe in my heart that You raised Jesus from the dead. I am putting my past life behind me and I close the door to Satan and any of his devices.

I thank You for forgiving me of all my sin. Jesus is my Lord and I am a new person. The old things have passed away and now all things have become new in Jesus' name. Amen.

Scripture References

John 3:16	John 14:6
John 6:37	Romans 10:9,10 NLT
John 10:10b	Romans 10:13
Romans 3:23	Ephesians 2:1-10 NCV
2 Corinthians 5:19	2 Corinthians 5:17
John 16:8,9	John 1:12
Romans 5:8	2 Corinthians 5:21

To Receive the Infilling of the Holy Spirit

Father, I am Your child because I believe in my heart that Jesus has been raised from the dead and I have declared with my mouth that He is my Lord.

Jesus said that the heavenly Father is ready to give the Holy Spirit to anyone who asks. I ask You now in the name of Jesus to fill me with the Holy Spirit. I step into the fullness and power that I desire in the name of Jesus.

Scripture References

John 14:16,17	Acts 10:44-46
Luke 11:13 NLT	Acts 19:2,5,6
Acts 1:8a	1 Corinthians 14:2-15
Acts 2:4	1 Corinthians 14:18,27
Acts 2:32,33,39	Ephesians 6:18
Acts 8:12-17	Jude 1:20

The Lord's Prayer

Our Father in heaven,
hallowed be your name,
your kingdom come,
your will be done ,
on earth as it is in heaven.
Give us today our daily bread.
And forgive us our debts,
as we also have forgiven our debtors.
And lead us not into temptation,
but deliver us from the evil one.

Matthew 6:9-13 NIV

About the Author

Germaine Griffin Copeland, founder and president of Word Ministries, Inc. is the bestselling author of the Prayers That Avail Much® family of books. Her writings provide scriptural prayer instruction to help you pray effectivly for those things that concern you and your family and for other prayer assignments.

Germaine is the daughter of the late Reverend A.H. "Buck" and Donnis Brock Griffin. She and her husband, Everette, have four children and eleven grandchildren. Their prayer assignments increase as great-grandchildren are born into the family. Germaine and Everette reside in Greensboro, Georgia.

Mission Statement
Word Ministries, Inc.

Motivating individuals to pray
Encouraging them to achieve intimacy with God
Bringing emotional wholeness and spiritual growth

You may contact Word Ministries by writing:
Word Ministries, Inc.
PO Box 289
Good Hope, Georgia 30641
www.prayers.org

*Please include your testimonies
and praise reports when you write.*

Other Books by Germaine Copeland

Prayers That Avail Much 25th Anniversary
Commemorative Hardbound Gift Edition

Prayers That Avail Much 25th Anniversary
Commemorative Leather Edition

Prayers That Avail Much
Commemorative Paperback Edition

Prayers That Avail Much Volume 1

Prayers That Avail Much Volume 2

Prayers That Avail Much Volume 3

Prayers That Avail Much for the Workplace

Prayers That Avail Much for Men - pocket edition

Prayers That Avail Much for Women - paperback

Prayers That Avail Much Women - pocket edition

Prayers That Avail Much for Mothers - paperback

Prayers That Avail Much for Moms - pocket edition

Prayers That Avail Much for Teens - hardback

Prayers That Avail Much for Teens - mass market

Prayers That Avail Much for the College Years

Oraciones Con Poder - Prayers That Avail Much
(Spanish Edition)

Available at fine bookstores everywhere
or from **www.harrisonhouse.com**

Fast. Easy.
Convenient.

For the latest Harrison House product information and author news, look no further than your computer. All the details on our powerful, life-changing products are just a click away. New releases, E-mail subscriptions, Podcasts, testimonies, monthly specials—find it all in one place. Visit harrisonhouse.com today!

harrisonhouse

The Harrison House Vision

Proclaiming the truth and the power

Of the Gospel of Jesus Christ

With excellence;

Challenging Christians to

Live victoriously,

Grow spiritually,

Know God intimately.